DATE DUE

MY 6 '97			
SE 2 '98			
OE 16 '08			

DEMCO 38-296

THE SPORTS
IMMORTALS

THE SPORTS IMMORTALS:
Deifying the
American Athlete

Peter Williams

Bowling Green State University Popular Press
Bowling Green, OH 43403

Sports and Culture

General Editors
Douglas Noverr
Lawrence Ziewacz

Other books in the series:

*Hunting and Fishing for Sport:
Commerce, Controversy, Popular Culture*
Richard Hummel

*Cricket for Americans:
A Beginner's Guide to Watching, Playing,
and Understanding the Game*
Tom Melville

*Baseball in 1889:
Players vs. Owners*
Daniel M. Pearson

Copyright © 1994 Bowling Green State University Popular Press

Library of Congress Catalog Card Number: 94-78929

ISBN: 0-87972-669-5 Clothbound
0-87972-670-9 Paperback

Cover design and type by Laura Darnell-Dumm

ACKNOWLEDGMENTS

I would chiefly like to thank the members of the Popular Culture Association, a group of entirely reasonable men and women who are always scholars but never academics, and, alphabetically and from within that large circle, especially these: Pat Browne, Ray Browne, Doug Noverr, Joe Price, Bruce Rubenstein, and Larry Ziewacz. I hope the many others I should have named will forgive my memory. Further, I'd like to thank Jim Kaplan, who published earlier versions of some of this material in *The Baseball Research Journal*; Mike Oriard, not only for his early encouragement, but also for his fine example in initiating professional studies like this one, and Pier Mancusi-Ungaro and Bonnie Herms Krassner, for directing me to much scholarship I might otherwise have missed. Last, I'd like to thank the following individuals, who will all understand why: Laura Gabrielsen, Beth Hess, Dee Jenkins, Ellen Mascia, Joe Mele, and Joe Vallely.

For

My daughter Maggie

Because she is always right

CONTENTS

PREFACE

I won't deny that the heavy majority of sportswriters, myself included, have been and still are guilty of puffing up the people they write about. I remember one time when Stanley Woodward, my beloved leader, was on the point of sending me a wire during spring training, saying, "Will you stop Godding up those ball players?" I didn't realize what I had been doing. I thought I had been writing pleasant little spring training columns about ball players.

If we've made heroes out of them, and we have, then we must also lay a whole set of false values at the doorsteps of historians and biographers. Not only has the athlete been blown up larger than life, but so have the politicians and celebrities in all fields, including rock singers and movie stars....

I've tried not to exaggerate the glory of athletes. I'd rather, if I could, preserve a sense of proportion, to write about them as excellent ball players, first-rate players. But I'm sure I have contributed to false values—as Stanley Woodward said, "Godding up those ball players."

—Red Smith

Red Smith was the best sports writer of our time, and Stanley Woodward was the best sports editor. Both worked in the sports department of the legendary *New York Herald-Tribune*, and when that writer heard that editor make that comment, he obviously both understood it and agreed with it. Red Smith also sounds as though he knows there was very little he could have done to change his reportorial habits.

The urge to "God up" persons we admire is as natural as it is myopic (or, more properly, telescopic), which is why we call such persons "idols." Smith himself points out that the process is not restricted to baseball, and figures of historical importance are mythified in exactly the same way as popular "stars." The accepted portrait of Beethoven has been a fixture

1

of a popular cartoon strip for several decades and is as essentially false as the icon of Elvis Presley on the stamp. George Washington never did chop down that cherry tree, and probably only Walter Johnson ever tossed a silver dollar across a wide river, but the real Washington is not the one we choose to believe in; we worship instead the grave face Gilbert Stuart gave us, the man who looks down on us from our currency like some grand old pharaoh.

This deifying mechanism has never been restricted to any particular place or time. Although it can never be proven, it seems very likely that Helen of Troy was little more than a zoftig Greek girl with a face capable of launching considerably fewer than a thousand ships, and that Hercules was only the Emil Sandow or "Hulk" Hogan of his day; even the devout may question the success the Welshman Patrick had with snakes, or the meek behavior of savage wolves in the presence of St. Francis. The impulse to "God up" humans is universal and inescapable, as much a part of our innate nature as the needs to love, eat, and sleep.

In this book I would like to examine how this human urge is worked out in sport, particularly in the relatively new and typically American sport of baseball. After a brief survey of the findings of the pioneers, the doctors, psychologists, and social scientists who first studied the phenomenon, I will look at how their theories are reflected in sport generally. Then I'll give a more detailed explanation of how these theories serve to explain how we have superimposed a myth over the history of baseball, creating in the process a sort of secular faith; finally I'll examine how we convert fact into fruitful fiction in other sports, and I'll conclude with a brief look at the role of the press in this process.

If Red Smith reacted to Stanley Woodward's exasperated crack with wry amusement, he would certainly have been tickled by a book like this, a serious effort to bring the likes of Otto Rank and Sir James George Frazer to bear on a kid's game; still, I think he would have understood the validity of a study which tries to explain why even his work simply could not avoid elevating the talented men he knew, transforming them into gods and heroes.

PART ONE

THE
THEORETICAL
FOUNDATION

INTRODUCTION:
PSYCHOLOGISTS
AND OTHER SOCIAL SCIENTISTS

Studies of the evolutionary development of the mind and behavior of man are necessarily suppositional, but it is possible to join a number of familiar hypotheses in a theory we might even call standard or accepted. Take the work of Adler and Freud on group psychology, for example; the former suggests that the physical inferiority of the individual in pre-human species resulted in our tendency to herd together socially, while the latter believes these pre-human groups, once formed, followed a single leader, the "alpha male" or "old man," and that this leader may have been the source of the idea of God. Fritz Redl's variation on Freud's view is slight but significant; he feels that by the time these early groups became human there was one central person, although not one who was necessarily a powerful leader. Then there is Johan Huizinga, in some ways the most interesting theorist for this study; he points out that all mammals play games of one kind or another, and wonders if this impulse to play, eventually inherited by the first humans, might actually lie behind human myths:

> In whatever form, from the most sacred to the most literary, from the Vedic Purusha to the fetching little figurines in the Rape of the Lock, personification is both a play-function and a supremely important habit of mind.... If this innate tendency of the mind, which invests the objects of ordinary life with personality, is in fact rooted in play then we are confronted with a very serious issue.... Would it therefore be overbold to suggest that the theriomorphic [beast-into-god] factor in ritual, mythology and religion can best be understood in terms of the play attitude? (140-41)

5

Granted, Huizinga is talking about gods who originate, not as humans, but as animals or even as things, whereas Freud and Redl talk of the direct deification of humans; still, as I hope to show, these are simply different methods of achieving the same mythic result. What is important is that all of these students of our very remote past agree there is a very good chance myth (and therefore myth-making) evolved even before we did.

Turning from the group to the individual, we can find a similar cohesion of different ideas, also resulting in a relatively "mainstream" theory, a theory, this time, of the psychic growth of each individual. Hernz Werner thinks perception and imagination were once a simple function in the pre-human mind, and that this explains the ease with which we now can move from the real to the mythic; Adler's emphasis on the physical inferiority of the pre-human individual leads him to the conclusion that we evolved intelligence for the same reason we began herding in groups, in order to survive. Both of these theories represent Darwinian efforts to understand how humans became dualistic, developing a mind alongside a body, moving above and beyond the simple perception and instinct of the lower animals. But the most important conjectures in this area are undoubtedly those made by Jung.

Like the others, Jung works his way back down the evolutionary ladder. There he finds the development of what he calls archetypes. Jung's archetypes don't actually exist, per se, in the human mind, at least not as recognizable images; what does exist there, and has existed since pre-human times, is the impulse to find or fulfill them:

> My critics have incorrectly assumed that I am dealing with "inherited representations," and on that ground they have dismissed the idea of the archetype as mere superstition.... [The archetypes] are, indeed, an instinctive trend, as marked as the impulse of birds to build nests, or ants to form organized colonies. (Man 58)

Jung calls these instinctive archetypes "primordial images" (*Two* 76), and he says they exist in the collective unconscious, and that they are "the residues of functions from man's animal ancestry" (109). Jung is not concerned here with the idea that we began thinking when imagination separated from perception, or because the principle of survival of the fittest made thought our only weapon against stronger biological groups; he believes that intelligence arose when our animal instinct began to pursue what he calls a proto-image, slowly creating the first body/mind, object/ subject dualism in the pre-human consciousness, and that these proto-images themselves gradually developed into archetypes. Once again, Jung is clear that he does not believe specific images are inherited; what is inherited, according to him, is the urge to locate and satisfy archetypes. The process by which we create manifestations of archetypal "forms" is innate, a pattern of behavior which has been forced on us and which, possibly more than any other, defines us as a species. The need to locate and realize archetypes is an urge we follow blindly, like salmon or lemmings.

If we move a little further along in pre-history, to the era of primitive man, we come to somewhat less chancy ground, since now there is some anthropological evidence on which to base conclusions. Freud, for example, looking at tribal myths, determines that there is a difference between sorcery, which seeks to propitiate and control gods, and magic, which purports to give men godlike power. Sir James George Frazer, looking in a similar direction, makes a similar distinction, although he opposes magic to a more limited kind of sorcery, one in which gods can be appeased, but only influenced, not controlled; Frazer calls that religion. As far as the creation of the gods themselves in these primitive cultures, they are always made by finding concrete manifestations for archetypal forms, by "filling" the eternal and universal archetypal "slots." Gods so created may be simply imagined, based on a concept, like love or power; they may be personified objects, made on analogy with nature, as Huizinga thinks, or they may be formed by "Godding up" some human model, which is the view of Freud. In other words, the first gods were imagined, metamorphosed, or transfigured, the form of the archetype being made incarnate in one of these ways.

Again, what is important here is the result, not the method. The ancients may have begun with a pretty girl, or a healthy crop of grain, or just the idea of fecundity in order to arrive at Demeter; the point is that any one of these methods would have resulted in some version of the same archetype. In fact, while the experts are in full agreement regarding the nature and significance of deities like Demeter, they are in no way sure of how she was made. Frazer, for example, maintains that her male counterpart Adonis was, pure and simple, the personification of annual planting and harvest of cereal grain (393-94); however, Frazer's most famous follower, Jessie Weston, refers to Sir W. Ridgeway's insistence that "Osiris, Attis, Adonis, were all at one time human beings, whose tragic fate gripped hold of popular imagination, and led to their ultimate deification," and Weston appears to side with Ridgeway (7-8). Whatever your dough, your cookie-cutter will make cookies of the same shape; the archetype remains constant, no matter what triggers its manifestation.

Now if you have gods, you probably have a system of faith, and a final word needs to be said about that. If, after the primitive era, sorcery gives way to religion, so also does science supersede what Frazer calls its "bastard sister," magic:

> Religion...clearly assumes that the course of nature is to some extent elastic or variable, and that we can persuade or induce the mighty beings who control it to deflect, for our benefit, the current of events from the channel in which they would otherwise flow. Now this implied elasticity or variability of nature is directly opposed to the principles of magic as well as of science, both of which assume that the processes of nature are rigid and invariable.... Thus in so far as religion assumes the world to be directed by conscious agents who may be turned from their purpose by persuasion, it stands in fundamental antagonism to magic as well as to science. (58-59)

The importance of this is that science, once it gained its foothold, was never going to lose favor, that it would remain "in fundamental antagonism" to religion, and that it would, by its very nature, as discovery succeeded discovery, inexorably gain in strength and influence. Eventually people starved for religion (and therefore for gods) and unable to accept substantially weakened conventional faiths would begin to create other, less sublime pantheons. They would have to, since to realize archetypes remained an essential part of their human nature; and that, of course, is what this book is about.

* * *

If the innate mythmaking impulse can be traced back through our history as a species, it can also be seen by examining the analogies to evolution in the growth of a human child. The first important theorist to connect the origins of myth with the development of the child was, unsurprisingly, Freud, who felt that helpless dependency makes every child view each parent as perfected divinity and embodiment of the sinless superego. As the child gets older, however, he becomes aware that his parents are imperfect; then, says Freud, he develops evasions (like "splitting" and "displacement," both of which serve to create fictional figures) in order to avoid confrontation with the parent/superego/god. In this way every child may create his own imagined mountaintop of Olympians. This view is not at all inconsistent with the theory of the Oedipus complex, in which the male child competes with a betraying father-god, and which may lead to the search for substitute parent-figures. In fact, Norman Brown has suggested that "the essence of the Oedipal complex is the project of becoming God," and, in quoting Brown's observation, Ernest Becker has connected that view with the human yearning for immortality (Otto Rank calls this yearning the "third principle") by saying that "the child wants to conquer death by becoming the father of himself" (36). Even Harold Bloom, applying the principle to writers, asks, "what strong maker desires the realization that he has failed to create himself?" (5) And Rank himself says this:

> The entire endeavor to replace the real father by a more distinguished one is merely the expression of the child's

longing for the vanished happy time, when his father still
appeared to be the strongest and greatest man and the
mother seemed the dearest and most beautiful woman....
Thus the overvaluation of the earliest years of childhood.
(71)

Ernest Becker has a fine phrase for what Rank calls the
"overvaluation" of these earliest years; with a significant
glance toward the myth of the fall, he calls it "the paradise
of prerepression" (64). Everything thereafter is, he says, a
denial, a game; for Becker, this appears with the greatest
clarity in the person who has "denied" just about everything,
the schizophrenic, in whose psyche we can find "the problem
of heroics in its stark nudity." Becker says the schizophrenic
himself is so lacking and in such need of a hero that "he has
to suck in an entire other human being to keep from
disappearing or flying away" (221). In all this Becker is in
part echoing R.D. Laing's thesis that the schizophrenic is
someone who indulges less in denial than the "normal"
human, whose ego is really, in Laing's phrase, a "false self."
For Becker, people create myth because they can't live with
reality. While the schizophrenic is obviously the most
extreme example of this repressive tendency, Becker says
what he calls "hero-transference" is much more prevalent. In
hero-transference, the individual surrenders partially to the
image of an idol, like the fan who dresses like a rock star or
the depression-era kid who carried his left arm twisted in the
manner of Carl Hubbell. Becker says that "man cannot stand
alone but has to reach out for support," and this kind of
transference is "a necessary projection in order to stand life,
death, and oneself" (158).

So even after they grow into repressed adults, humans
never lose the capacity to make myth. In Jung's view, for
instance, the impulse to harmonize all his disparate psychic
aspects will lead a mature individual to the conception of a
perfect god, one who then appears at the center of the
mandala, Jung's quasi-mystical echo of Leonardo's drawing of
man; it can be argued that this is what happened to Walt
Whitman when he called himself a "kosmos," and the notion
is supported by the fact that Walt's godlike self is at the
absolute center of his work (a parallel example would be

Joyce's *Finnegans Wake*, whose hero is both a specific individual and a kosmos-encompassing god). As always, however, the most important part of Jung's approach to myth is the theory of archetypes:

> The unconscious contains, as it were, two layers: the personal and the collective.... The collective layer comprises the pre-infantile period, that is, the residues of ancestral life.... The archetypes of the collective unconscious are not filled out because they are forms not personally experienced.... When psychic energy regresses, going even beyond the period of early infancy, and breaks into the legacy of ancestral life, then mythological images are awakened: these are the archetypes.... The idea of God is an absolutely necessary psychological function of an irrational nature, which has nothing whatever to do with the question of God's existence.... The idea of an all-powerful divine Being is present everywhere, unconsciously if not consciously, because it is an archetype. (*Two* 87, 81)

As Ira Progoff has pointed out, "kollectiv" in German is much closer in meaning to "inherently human" than is our "collective," and inherently human is precisely the meaning Jung wants to convey when he talks about that level of the unconscious that preserves and contains the archetypes. These archetypes are the inherently human patterns, the platonic forms of the science of the mind. They are as fully and as inevitably "in" people as the ability to recognize a natural predator is "in" a young animal who has never before seen that predator; archetypes seem closely related to what biologists call IRMs (Innate Releasing Mechanisms), the inherited triggers that teach the rabbit to run from the hawk. It is clear why Jung's archetypes are of such vital importance to any study of myth.

This is not to discredit the similar importance of the views of Otto Rank. Although his "third principle" is less firmly based in the physical sciences than are Jung's archetypes, it remains hard to dispute, even if only because it seems so well supported by common sense. Rank says, simply, that we all, in one way or another, wish we could live forever, and that each era gives this wish a different form, resulting in a "dominant immortality ideology" for every historical period. An individual's immortality may be achieved in the continuance of his group, in the endless survival of himself, or in the monumental permanence of some work or deed done by the individual. The third principle is really just a different way of saying, with Becker, that we all "deny" the certainty of death. As Becker points out, Kierkegaard comes to very similar conclusions; so does Miguel de Unamuno, who says that "not dying" is "the supreme human need" (319) and suggests that the fear of pain after death is never the issue:

> I remained unmoved when shown the most moving pictures of hell, for even then nothing appeared to me quite so horrible as nothingness itself. It was a furious hunger of being that possessed me. (9)

No doubt we could find illustrations just as pointed in death-conscious writers from Lucretius to Beckett, but suffice it to say that the wish for immortality codified in Rank's third principle seems itself to be archetypal.

*   *   *

I have tried to point out that all of these pioneer students of myth present theories sufficiently similar that they can be said to be in general agreement, and that such disagreement as does exist is largely irrelevant, since it deals with how the archetypes of myth were created, not with what they are. Again, although Frazer and Weston disagree on the origins of Adonis, they are in accord regarding the archetypal figure of Adonis himself. Further, although each man has his own distinct theory, it can hardly be denied that Rank, Becker, and Unamuno are right in saying we don't want to die, that Freud accurately shows we must eventually become disillusioned with our parents, and that Jung's archetypes (supported as they are by both anthropology and biology) are virtually impossible to dismiss. What remains is to attempt to catalog the primary figures and patterns we may call archetypal, those characters, plots, and other elements which continue to recur both regularly and universally.

Chapter 1

THE ARCHETYPES OF HUMAN MYTH

Archetypes need not be anthropomorphic, gods like Demeter and Adonis; they can also be stories, locations (like Arcadia, Utopia, Valhalla or the Underworld), things (like a magic branch or wand) or even abstract and conceptual, like the fear of falling asleep and falling out of a tree. I would like to suggest that five categories of archetypes of various kinds are particularly relevant to the study of myth. These are archetypal figures, narrative and agonistic archetypes, and finally archetypes of place and archetypal tools.

Archetypes of place are settings which recur in myth, and archetypal tools are devices (either physical or conceptual, and nearly always magical) used by mythical characters to gain their goals. By archetypal figures I mean the anthropomorphic figures of the gods and heroes of myth, and by agonistic archetypes I mean those gods and heroes when they are in conflict with one another; when they are, a different set of archetypal "labels" applies, as a god can look quite different in a suit of armor. Conflict invites ethical distinction; for example, either a wily trickster (Shakespeare's Iago) or a powerful figure (his Macbeth) can "fill" a new agonistic "slot," that of villain. Finally, narrative archetypes are the plots of myth, and it is with these I would like to begin.

A. Narrative: The Archetypal Journey

Ah, dearo! Dearo, dear! And her illian! And his willyum! When they were all there now.... And then and too the trivials! And their bivouac! And his monomyth! Ah ho!
—James Joyce
(*Finnegans Wake* 581)

15

Joseph Campbell borrowed Joyce's coinage "monomyth" to label his version of the archetypal heroic plot. Campbell's version has three main stages, separation, initiation and return. In the first, the hero is called, refuses the call, meets a protector, and crosses a threshold. In the second, he passes a test, often given by a goddess, and there are four likely events: his sacred marriage, atonement with his father, his apotheosis, and his theft of an elixir. In the last stage, the hero either refuses to return or is unable to until he gets help, although his return, when it is accomplished, may present him with problems.

While Campbell's is one of the best-known accounts of the "stations" of the archetypal myth, it is far from the only one. Rank himself lists several stages in *The Myth of the Birth of the Hero*, and Lord Raglan says each hero has twenty-two "features," many of which match stages in Campbell's list (Raglan's hero will marry a princess and become a king; Campbell's will have a sacred marriage and experience an apotheosis). Vladimir Propp lists thirty-one "functions" in the archetypal narrative, and he says they must always occur in the same sequence. Propp divides his plot into six stages, not three; preparation, complication, and transference (Campbell's "separation"), struggle (Campbell's "initiation"), and return, then recognition (Campbell's "return"). Further, Propp's "functions" often match Raglan's "features" closely. Two things are evident here: the narrative of the archetypal heroic myth is always the same, and the number of significant events in the story will vary only according to how much detail the mythographer wants to provide.

We can look at archetypal narrative in another way, however: as a grafting of two myths, both of vital concern to us. The most obvious of these two is the quest myth, and, although it can be argued that the monomyth is already a quest, I think the real quest only begins after Campbell's "separation"; the other myth, always associated with that separation, is the myth of the loss of paradise, and that story is often forgotten in the excitement of the later hunt.

If we view the "monomyth" as not tripartite, but actually binary, or as folded over on itself, I think we do its significance more justice: then it becomes a pattern, not just for the Homeric or Hegelian man of action, but for every man, involving as it does growth from original innocence into knowledge, and then a return (triumphant or otherwise) to the point of origin. If one manifestation of the archetypal narrative is the quest for the Grail, another is surely Voltaire's *Candide*, in which an enlightened hero returns to a starting point of sorts. This expulsion-return model seems well suited to a number of myths, from the double epic of Homer (Ulysses leaves home in the first book and returns there in the second) to Wordsworth's notion that the very old can recapture the divine vision of the very young. On the most fundamental level, of course, the two-part model parallels the trauma of birth and the subsequent urge to return to the womb.

For these reasons, I propose to make the division of the archetypal narrative simpler, not more cumbersome. I view the story as having not three, but two main parts, the journey outward (innocence, expulsion or separation, condemnation or abandonment) and the trip back (experience or knowledge, reunion, forgiveness or rediscovery). It is during both of these journeys that the hero is tested, those tests determining whether his quest will be successful; in my view the climax is the point at which the outward motion is reversed and the return begins, and it coincides with final loss of innocence and attainment of knowledge.

B. Setting: Stages on the Archetypal Journey

There are two broad categories of mythical setting (or of any setting, for that matter): the architectural and the natural. Architectural settings (the temple, the city) are what Nietzsche calls Apollonian, and chiefly reflect what Jung says is our rational animus; natural ones (the garden, the grove or forest) are, in Nietzsche's term, Dionysiac, and correspond more to Jung's emotional anima.

These terms (which I will use throughout this study), and which are also related to the Eastern yang and yin, correspond to the reasonable and emotional parts of the bicameral human psyche. While purists may accuse me of nonchalance in my tendency to use them interchangeably, the fact is that I am using these terms in their broadest senses, to describe the most general differences between the two sides of every human personality. The significant point here is not that Jung, Nietzsche, and the Oriental philosophers hold different views regarding the complexity of human nature, rather that, beneath the differences, the similarities are so great.

But to return to mythical settings: they are often purely pastoral, or Arcadian, but they can become more complex. While an Arcadian place is simply natural, completely unified settings involve harmonious combination, with orderly buildings placed reasonably in an organic, bucolic scene. Since this joining of urban and pastoral, which also joins Apollonian or animus to Dionysiac or anima, takes an ideal form, I will call such settings Utopias.

There is authoritative precedent to use the term in that way. In Utopia itself, More put a number of cities on a spacious island; they are all walled, towered, and square in shape, but they are all also surrounded by delightful nature, backed by hills, with river and ocean nearby. Two decades later, Rabelais decorated *his* Utopia, the hexagonal Abbey of Theleme, with six identical round towers; but he also made sure it came with a pleasure garden, an orchard, and a great park. Both of these famous ideal locales are indebted to the medieval land of Cockayne, although the abbey there housed monks who were even more rowdy than those of Rabelais.

In fact, Cockayne and Theleme (which has no clocks) both also illustrate a frequent feature of utopias (Voltaire's El Dorado and James Hilton's Shangri-La also come to mind): their happy citizens have a great deal of difficulty either aging or dying. And, of course, this absence of time and decay is the chief hallmark of the most powerful myth of this sort, although, since it lacks architecture, it is only pastoral and arcadian and not fully utopian: that of paradise in Eden.

A word should be added here about a particularly useful visual illustration of these ideas, Jung's mandala. The mandala diagrams the complementary harmony of animus and anima. In one of its most basic forms, it shows the figure of an individual at the center of both a square and a circle (again, think of Leonardo's famous drawing, in which he depicts man in exactly that fashion). The corners of the square represent the conflicting elements of the self, while the circle stands for the harmony they achieve in a balanced psyche. The mandala is often found in architecture, and particularly in ideal or utopian buildings; for instance, it is found in the hexagonal form (both round and cornered) of Rabelais' abbey. The importance of the architectural manifestation of the mandala to this study will become apparent later.

Utopias not only reconcile contraries physically, they do the same thing socially. Citizens of these places are always just as much concerned with the well-being of others as they are with their own. If utopian monks observe Theleme's motto (DO AS YOU WILL), they also respect the Benedictine Rule ("let all things be common to all, nor let anyone say that anything is his own"). This perfect combination of selfishness and charity is the fullest expression of the golden rule; "you," in the utopian reading, gets as much as "others."

The utopian setting, then, builds on the pastoral and arcadian one by adding architecture to nature; as Wallace Stevens would say, once you combine order with organism, the wilderness, although still there, is no longer wild. The people lucky enough to live there find that it is difficult or impossible to age and that they are uniformly happy; they live by simultaneously satisfying their own desires and respecting those of others, and they are able to do both without experiencing any conflict.

Finally, it is certainly obvious that the completed Utopia shares many qualities (like happiness and relative death-lessness) with the pastoral paradise, the *locus amoenus* or "delightful place" of Arcadia. I think this can be explained if we match these archetypal places to my reading of the archetypal myth.

Take Samuel Johnson's *Rasselas*. When Rasselas leaves Abyssinia's Happy Valley, he is leaving a place of innocence, and he leaves in search of knowledge; when he comes back, he returns to Abyssinia, but there is no mention of any return to the Happy Valley. Or look at Adam and Eve—they leave their first paradise after eating from the Tree of

Knowledge; when they reach their second, they will no longer be naive. Similarly, Blake's innocent children must go through the fire of experience in order to reach wisdom, when they will see that both the lamb and the tyger are part of the same whole, and Wordsworth's child must grow old before he can reclaim the vision of glory he lost in early youth. The self of Kierkegaard, Unamuno, Laing, and Becker must find ways of dealing with an adult world which introduces that self to the certainty of death; if those ways are found, the self will have reclaimed a measure of contentment, a return of sorts to the happy time.

In other words, the archetypal hero is expelled from Arcadia, but his quest is to return and find it transformed into Utopia: Utopia, which adds understanding to instinct, represents a merging of the Apollonian and Dionysiac sides of human nature, and it is the place sought out by our mature wisdom.

Lastly, mention must be made of the two important archetypal places which lie outside the quest. The Underworld, often visited by the quester, is where failed heroes go after the quest; the world of celestial reward (I'll call it Valhalla) is where the successful hero is honored after the quest. Although these two places are extraneous to the monomyth proper, they do have considerable importance, as we'll see.

C. Dramatis Personae: The Archetypal Figures

The Freudian suggestion that the first "gods" each child recognizes are his parents is borne out (or at least paralleled) by the universal phenomenon of two all-encompassing gods, the omnipotent male and the great mother. These are the most complete gods. While the only entirely "complete" god would be hermaphroditic, these two, when taken together, complement each other so as to harmonize the human opposites of thought and instinct, and to merge power with fecundity, thus reflecting the psychic unity represented by anima and animus in Jung's mandala. Despite the fact that they seem so perfectly balanced, however, usually only one of these great deities is ascendent in any given era. Jahweh is male, and so is Allah, and even Zeus seemed to have the final say in his disputes with Hera, but the earliest human societies were often matriarchal, elevating the great mother to the position of Olympian leadership. Erich Neumann says these matriarchal societies were characterized by a "universal symbolic formula," which he gives as this:

Woman=body=vessel=world

Therefore in worshipping the great mother, we were worshipping the world.

The central symbol for the great mother, says Neumann, is the vessel, and he talks about the powerful archetype which preceded the great female god and which he calls the "Great Round" and the "Great Container." Humans respond to this archetype like children, he says, and even as adults we are unable to escape the influence of the mother-god:

> The Great Container tends to hold fast to everything that springs from it and to surround it like an eternal substance. Everything born of it belongs to it and remains subject to it; and even if the individual becomes independent, the Archetypal Feminine relativizes this independence into a nonessential variant of her own perpetual being. (25)

Another quality of the great mother, and one not found in the omnipotent father, is what Neumann calls the "participation mystique," the relationship between goddess and devotee, which is also analogous to that between mother and child, and which Neumann says is "the original situation of container and contained" (29). While at first it seems hard to imagine how the great container/great mother archetype could be relevant to myth-making in our modern male-dominated society, and particularly in the very male-dominated area of sport, I hope to show that she remains very much with us—as indeed she must, if she's a genuine archetype.

The parent/god archetypes, of course, are the broadest and most comprehensive we have, the biggest "forms" into which we pour our natural myth-building energy. They also reflect a central quality of myth, its dualistic character. "A noticeable characteristic of mythical stories is their markedly binary aspect," says Edmund Leach; "myth is constantly setting up opposing categories" (2).

Those "opposing categories" always are, however, as much complementary as contradictory: yin and yang, the "paired opposites" Jung speaks of, or the "shadows" mentioned by both Jung and Roland Barthes. This need for "shadows," which are like negative images in photography, could explain why a truly hermaphroditic god never caught on, why the first great divine figures were given gender; the phrase *vive la difference* may have connotations much deeper and more primal than we know.

In any event, myth continued its binary bias even after Zeus and Hera were lodged on their mountaintop. Each of these figures, the omnipotent male and the great mother, split, and the pairs that resulted were further divided until at last we had a thriving community of lesser gods, each with his or her own particular talent, specialty or job description. Since the gods so divided remained intact in the process, the result was a hierarchy not unlike that explained to Dante by St. Bernard in the Paradiso: Zeus, in other words, has some of Ares in him, but also some of Apollo; Hera will "contain" qualities associated with both Aphrodite and Artemis. While I propose to be neither comprehensive nor mathematically oversimple in discussing the archetypal personal categories that result from all this meiosis, I do hope to come up with a viable rack of archetypal costumes which will represent the roles humans most need to both adopt themselves and to impose on their peers.

Turning first to the great mother, we will see that she splits into two secondary types, the "good" and the "terrible" mother, and that these archetypes are also "shadows" of each other in which we can see Jung's anima (body and emotion) opposed to his animus (reason and inspiration). There is no paradox here, incidentally; even though the great mother takes on the anima role when coupled with the animus of the great father, taken by herself she still has a good deal of animus in her, just as the father has his anima side; Jung, who clearly says that both elements exist in both the male and the female psyche, would view the two great divinities as similarly complex.

At any rate, the good mother is the life-giver, the container that bears young; the terrible mother devours. The vessel of the "great round" can be a womb, or it can be a pit; it can be a kiln, or a yawning grave. The archetype of the terrible mother is filled with figures connected with evil or death (Medusa, Hecate), while the good mother is represented by those associated with virtue or life (Mary, Demeter).

This dichotomy offers a particularly clear historical illustration of how myth-making both builds upon and totally disregards the real individual. Is Joan of Orleans Saint Joan, Joan of the rainbow, the untouched virgin and stand-in for the Mother of God, or is she Joan la Pucelle, the whore, the witch they burned at Rouen? She comes down to us as either, depending upon whether you're reading Shakespeare or Twain; it seems her contemporaries created two concurrent myths, which, for a while at least, were popular rivals. The sexual contrast in Joan's case is particularly significant: the good mother, like Mary, bears life without sex; the terrible one, the vagina dentata, uses sex to destroy life. The notion that sex is destructive to the male (which conception may itself be an archetype) can be seen in everything from the Elizabethan use of the verb "to die" as synonymous with "to ejaculate" to Sterling Hayden's mad General Ripper in *Dr. Strangelove*, who never has sex because women want to kill him by stealing his "bodily fluids."

The great father-god develops two aspects, too, and they are best described by Nietzsche in his contrast of Apollo, the god of balance, order and restraint, to Dionysus, the god of formless and sometimes savage energy. Although it would be wrong to make a completely rigorous comparison, Apollo does resemble the good mother, and can be said to embody Jung's animus, while Dionysus looks a lot like the terrible mother, and certainly seems to contain the qualities of Jung's anima. The Dionysiac is essentially physical, and is characterized by strength; the spiritual Apollonian is identified by qualities of mind.

Before going any further, however, a very crucial point must be made: despite labels like "good" and "terrible," or "rational" and "savage," these categories are not ethically based, any more than Shelley's west wind is better for being a "preserver" than for being a "destroyer." The opposed qualities of the divided great mother and great father are simply further binary reflections of our own dualistic nature, of our bicameral mind; the archetypes will be given ethical flavoring only after some form of conflict surfaces among them, when they enter the agonistic phase.

Having moved down the divine genealogical chart from the hermaphroditic proto-god to the omnipotent father and the great mother, and then to these secondary pairs of male and female gods, we are ready to look at the final level, the level which will contain most of the recognizable personal archetypes. As I've said, the number of identifiable archetypes is potentially enormous, if not infinite; it depends on where you draw the line. In the interest of a simplicity which I believe will not weaken my argument, I'd like to suggest six more categories, all on the male side of the divine ledger, since that side will necessarily be more pertinent in the sexist arena of sport. In my scheme, the Dionysiac figure has three incarnations, and so does the Apollonian. The productive or directed Dionysiac is a successful strong man who puts his strength to good use. He is the hero who uses his energy to achieve his goal, like the Achilles of Homer's *Iliad*, but he has two "shadows": one is the failure, the Dionysiac who directs his power towards his goal, but who simply isn't strong enough to achieve it (Hector in the *Iliad*); the other is the destructive or misdirected Dionysiac, who has the strength to reach his goal but who uses his strength in service of the wrong end (Orestes in Aeschylus' *Oresteia*, or Macbeth in Shakespeare's play). The destructive Dionysiac, in destroying his hopes, often also destroys himself.

Similarly, an Apollonian with little sense of balance and order (i.e., judgment) is a fool, the shadow of the traditionally productive "wise" Apollonian. The third division of Apollonian is the thinker who is more wily than solomonic, the trickster. He also succeeds by using his mind, but his success is achieved through craft. He is the con-artist; the fool is the mark.

Now I think it would be sensible to take a brief time out to illustrate my system by applying it to two well-known literary myths. In Molière's *Tartuffe*, the eponymous Apollonian crafty trickster nearly defeats Orgon, the Apollonian fool, despite the best efforts of Cléante, the Apollonian sage; the truth is ultimately revealed as a result of a trick played by one of the other crafty Apollonians, Eliante, but the day is not saved until the intervention of the messenger of the King, who is, as great father, as high as you can get on the archetypal charts (Molière is undoubtedly right not to try to put this archetype on the stage). Or take Shakespeare's *Othello*, which is of interest because both the hero, Othello, and the heroine, Desdemona, are not heroic at all, archetypally speaking; they are fools, and their folly dooms them both. Of course, Othello is more than just a fool—he is, at different times, both a sage and a destructive Dionysiac—showing that a single individual can get into a plural number of archetypal costumes in the course of the same story. What makes the play particularly tragic is that it is hard to see how Othello could have been transformed into fool and destructive Dionysiac had he not been matched against one of the most accomplished tricksters in the history of myth. Othello also gives us one character who has the distinction of being both Apollonian fool and Dionysiac failure, the thoroughly unappealing Roderigo.

Our next step is to recognize that any of these six archetypal figures may appear in one of six significant variations. In two of these, the figure is forced out of the myth; in two, he is affected by time; in two he either changes, or appears to change, his archetypal role. The figures who do move from one archetype to another, like Lucifer or Mary Magdalene, are often models of damnation and redemption; the figures who only seem to change, like Prince Hal at the end of Shakespeare's *Henry IV*, or Nora at the end of Ibsen's *A Doll's House*, are really just a subtler variety of trickster. Regarding figures affected by time, it must be remembered that the standard image of the archetype is always a mature adult, never a child and never elderly—a glance at most classical statuary will show the truth of this—therefore it represents a departure from the archetypal norm when a figure is shown as either very young or very old. Finally, when the archetypal figure is discarded, we have either the outcast (or pariah) or the martyr, possibly the most important variations on the archetypal persons.

Martyrs and Pariahs

If martyrs are the tragic victims of fate, pariahs are the justly expelled, those properly punished by God. The best example of pariah is probably Cain. The classical era provides the best models for the martyr in Adonis and Persephone, and this archetype is particularly powerful because it echoes the seasonal pattern of birth, death, and rebirth. This has been most extensively treated by Frazer in his discussion of the story of Adonis and his compeers within the martyr's archetype, and it can, like any of the other three, combine with any of the figures on my initial list. For example, Othello, Desdemona, and Joan are all martyrs, despite their other archetypal differences.

Youth and Age

Regarding archetypal figures who appear either as children or as old people, it must be noted that this kind of variation sometimes creates in us a different response to the figure. For example, the strong and productive Dionysiac who wins in combat is more admirable if he is weakened either by childhood or age; we like the Biblical child David better than the adult Achilles, and even the officer who affirms that Shakespeare's old King Lear did in fact kill Cordelia's killer sounds impressed. Similarly, a very young wise figure, such as Christ in the temple or Mozart, will seem more admirable than an old one. This is not to say that the process can't work in reverse: we forgive Huck Finn his innocent mistakes, but in the case of his father—well, there's no fool like an old fool; and when confronted with stupidity, we are likely to find it even more pitiable as childhood moves into age, as with Benjy in Faulkner's *The Sound and the Fury* or Lennie in Steinbeck's *Of Mice and Men*. The most common effect the extremes of both youth and age have on all archetypal figures, however, is to increase our sympathy for them.

Role-Changing or Mask-Wearing

The last two variations on my archetypal figures are the role-changers and the mask-wearers. These two variations, while not in themselves ethically defined, lend themselves more easily than the others to our moral judgment: the role-changers, who have found new codes of living, tend to be judged according to those individual choices; the mask-wearers, who by definition fool others, are often judged according to their motives in regard to the others they fool. Regarding the former, I've mentioned those who change from selfless to dissolute (Lucifer) or those who, like Magdalene, reverse that process. Of course, the role-changer need not be an ethical example, a figure fallen or saved; in Ibsen's play, Nora moves from fool to sage, and that's not a matter of ethics. Regarding mask-wearers, in addition to the examples already given, think of Iago, who is repeatedly called "honest" during the course of *Othello*, although the only time he is is when he tells us "I am not what I am"; Iago is a crafty trickster wearing the mask of a sage. So, usually, is Tartuffe (although not during his blunt proposition of Eliante), and certainly one of the most common instances of mask-wearing is the con man pretending to be upright. Still, figures wearing the costumes of their "shadows" probably appear in all the archetypal categories. Shakespeare's Prince Hal has already been mentioned. Hal is an upright and sagacious Apollonian pretending to be both a fool and a destructive Dionysiac. Falstaff, in the same play, reverses this; he pretends to kill Hotspur, and is the destructive Dionysiac pretending to be a strong and productive one. The Fool in *Lear* is really a sage in motley, and there is certainly no shortage of *real* fools pretending to be wise. The terrible mother masquerading as the good was common in medieval tales (think of Spenser's *Faerie Queene*, and of Duessa, or duplicity, convincing the virtuous knight that she's really Fidessa, or fidelity).

In this connection, I can't resist citing a remarkable contemporary instance of mask-wearing in which the sexually destructive terrible mother wears the mask of the Holy Virgin: I shouldn't have to add that I'm speaking of the rock star Madonna. Interestingly, when the satirist Julie Brown parodied Madonna in a short film, she yanked off the singer's mask by re-naming her *Medusa.* It must be stressed that this is a *precise* echo of what happens in more conventionally "serious" myths—for example, in Spenser, when the apparently beautiful Duessa's reptilian body is revealed to the Court by Prince Arthur.

D. Spells and Weapons: The Archetypal Tools

The archetypal figures who act out the monomyth and its variations use devices in their attempts to achieve their goals, "tools" which can range from weapons to incantations, and which usually have magical properties. While these tools are important parts of the archetypal narrative, they are also symbols. If we follow Freud, they are symbols created on analogy with perceived reality; if we follow Jung, they are imagined, created from a need to concretize a concept. Again, it hardly matters, since the result remains the same. Take the sword Excalibur. Freud would say it was a symbolic representation of the penis; Jung would say it was the physical correlative of the idea of potency. Either way, of course, Excalibur both symbolizes the strength of the King and serves as a major device in the telling of his tale.

The sword in general is one of the most persistently recurrent archetypal tools in myth, possibly for Jung's reasons as well as those of Freud, and it has its counterpart in the container (note that Zeus wields the ultimate sword, the bolt of lightning, and that his wife is the incarnation of Neumann's "Great Container"). Jessie Weston calls these two archetypes the lance and the cup, noting how vital they are to the myth of the Holy Grail, but also pointing out that they "were in truth connected together in symbolic relation long ages before the institution of Christianity, or the birth of Celtic tradition," and that they "are sex symbols of immemorial antiquity and world-wide diffusion, the Lance, or Spear, representing the Male, the Cup, or Vase, the Female, reproductive energy" (75). In addition to their symbolic value, though, archetypal tools are always of practical value to the hero as he pursues his goal, and, as I've noted, they are normally magical. If the typical "lance," like Excalibur, contains magic, so does the typical "cup," the Grail, as any moviegoer familiar with the Monty Python troupe can attest.

A few more categories of magical tools need to be mentioned. First, there are those directly associated with a particular lost deity. These are *relics*, and anyone who has visited the cathedrals of Europe knows how important they once were. To pick one example, the bones of Mary Magdalene are scattered all over not just the countryside, but the continent; I myself have seen parts of her in three churches, Vézelay in northern France, Ste. Maximin in Provence, and Oviedo in Spain. That relics in their heyday were not viewed as genuine by everyone is made plain by Chaucer, whose Pardoner admits his are only animal bones. Still, people worshiped them and the power thought to be in them, and a visit to one of these cathedrals today will show you that the practice continues. Even Chaucer's Pardoner, after admitting they're fake, asks the other pilgrims to pay him for the privilege of kissing his "relics," and he nearly gets away with it. But we are dealing with myth, not history, and, as Becker points out, one of the creative forces behind myth is simple denial.

Relics are *particular* tools, in that there can be only one of each; *general* tools are those objects imbued with magic which have never been associated with the saints or deities addressed. There are three basic kinds. The individual may have either an amulet, which will ward off evil (the cross and Dracula), or a talisman, which will actively bring good (Aladdin's lamp, the rabbit's foot); the group may have a palladium, which will protect them as long as it is in their possession (the statue of Pallas Athene in Troy). Finally, there is the "tool" (in that it also helps the hero achieve his goal) of the incantation, spell, or magical rite: Faust calling up Mephistopheles; the three girls torturing Jack Nicholson in the film, *The Witches of Eastwick*; sacrifice, eating a particular animal, facing in a particular direction (often east), the various ceremonies of worship itself.

Chapter 2

LOCALIZED ARCHETYPES

A. Place, Time and Cultural Group

To "read" a pantheon is to read a culture's sense of itself.
— David Leeming
(*The World of Myth* 95)

The public has adopted the celebrity as an image of a certain kind and expects him to perform the functions of that image.... The "rights" of the public over its image include the privilege of using the celebrity as a scapegoat.
— Orrin Klapp
(*Symbolic Leaders* 17-18)

I have been dealing so far with the attributes of the monomyth, those events, characters, settings and tools which are represented always and everywhere. Now I'd like to try to locate myth in particular cultures. Any specific culture is "located" both historically and geographically, of course, defined by both space and time, and the first and biggest division of the monomyth into local versions probably occurred when distinct cultural differences began to develop between East and West. No one was ever more aware of the importance of mythical archetypes than Joyce, as *Finnegans Wake* makes plain, and in *Ulysses* he emphasizes the importance of the contrast between East and West by having Bloom represent the Orient, Stephen the Occident; in this opposition, Bloom is given many more "female" attributes, and resembles Jung's anima, whereas the compulsively rational student-philosopher Stephen is much closer to Jung's *animus*.

Joyce's contrast is anything but revolutionary: we have long considered Eastern myth to be more concerned with unity, Western with rational division, just as Brahma encompasses and unifies the Eastern world, while the Christian god (itself divided) is above and apart from humanity. Owen Barfield, commenting on this essential difference, points out that the West tends to "add" up separate ways of seeing and understanding, differentiating them, while the East will "absorb" them into a whole vision, one which remains always an indivisible unity (221-22). As Joyce's emphasis on this contrast implies, the eastern is a "shadow"—a negative but complementary image—of the western version of the monomyth.

When you further subdivide either East or West into particular cultures, you'll find that each culture's myth may define that culture in up to four ways: politically, socially, ethically, and psychologically. When the monomyth is located in a particular place and time, it will illustrate that local culture in those ways, telling us how the people there thought and behaved individually, socially, and ethically. Further, since no culture is monolithic, there will be sub-cultures which, having their own values, will have their own variants on the local myth. While blacks in America are currently deifying Malcolm X more than ever, whites still prefer to sanctify King, this despite the fact that both men "fill" the same archetypal "slots," those of Apollonian sage and Adonic martyr. A good example of a sub-culture's revision of a dominant culture's myth is the Sudanese writer Tayib Salih's *Season of Migration to the North*. In Salih's book, which is a serious parody of Joseph Conrad's *Heart of Darkness*, the hero, in Edward Said's words, "voyages into the heart of light, which is modern Europe, and discovers there what has been hidden deep within him" (43). Conrad's novel represents the primary Western myth, while Salih's looks at it through a lens made in the Third World.

We can see particular locations and sub-groups in time, too: Nathaniel Hawthorne, writing in Salem, Massachusetts, also wrote *of* Salem, but of a culture two centuries gone, and the ironic tension of his fiction results from the fact that his judgments are very different from those of his great-grandfather; and, as Jorge Luis Borges has mischievously shown in "Pierre Menard, Author of the Quixote," if that novel had been written in our century, it would be a very different book. The fashionable critical school called New

Historicism bases its conclusions on ideas like these: everybody liked Ike in the '50s, although now he seems a bland anachronism; Joe Louis was a national icon in the '40s, but by the '60s he had become a Tom, moving from the archetype of productive Dionysiac to that of Apollonian fool. In other words, while the archetypes are always universal, they also must always be read in context, on the positional grid of place and time, and according to the local cultural standards that place and time mandate.

B. The Archetypal Agon

Finally, if local myths are plural, they must necessarily be competitive. It's hard to think of a disastrous human conflict, from the classical era down through the Crusades and up to and beyond the October Revolution, that has not been fought under the banners of competing myths. Each side, of course, thinks their myth is true, the other myth false; to each side, the opposing god is really the devil (see the Roman Catholic Dante's treatment of the Muslim Mohammed). Although the shadow-figures of the central myth imply conflict, it is not inherent in the scheme; the trickster does not *have* to become the villain; there is no real separation of bad and good guys on Olympus. Ethics do not really enter into myth until the monomyth has divided and re-located in different cultures, thus creating teams with different mascots and rooters of different persuasions. At any rate, and since competition will be so central to what follows, I'd like to offer another group of archetypal figures, ones that represent the figures I've already mentioned when those figures become embattled with their counterparts from a neighboring myth. I have borrowed these six archetypes from Étienne Souriau, although Vladimir Propp, working independently, developed a very similar list:

1. *Hero* (Propp uses two types, hero and donor)
2. *Rival* (Propp uses two types, villain and false hero)
3. *Goal* (Propp personifies this "desired object" as Princess)
4. *Receiver of Goal* (Propp has no clearly apposite category)
5. *Judge* (Propp has no clearly apposite category)
6. *Helper* (Propp uses two types, helper and dispatcher)

It should be noted that none of these figures are necessary matches for the archetypes of the central myth. This is primarily because they are *dramatic* archetypes, forms of modes of *action*; they appear only when there is some kind of conflict or agon, and then virtually any of the archetypes I've listed can serve any of Souriau's six functions. As an example, think of Iago, who is an archetypal trickster who does not become a "bad guy" until he enters the agonistic conflict, whereupon he also becomes a villain (or false hero); had he used his considerable craft in a different cause, he might well have become a hero, like the good magician Prospero in Shakespeare's *The Tempest*.

These agonistic categories can show how located myths differ from one another, how different cultures may force the same person into different archetypal roles. Take the saga of the Trojan War. Looking at archetypal figures, Achilles is a productive Dionysiac and Hector is a failed one, while Ulysses, although he has Dionysiac strength, is primarily a crafty Apollonian; Helen combines the undirected energy of a destructive Dionysiac with the unwisdom of the fool and the helplessness of the Adonic martyr. Despite the ethical implications in the characters as thus described (and these may be culturally localized), the story doesn't become a blatantly moral one until Virgil writes his response to Homer in the *Aeneid*, creating the conflict between two views of the universal myth. Then (in Virgil) Hector becomes Souriau's hero, Achilles becomes the rival (Propp's villain), and the worthy trickster Ulysses, now only a con-artist, also becomes a rival (this time, Propp's false hero). Helen becomes only Souriau's impersonal "goal," which is perhaps as it should be, since she was always only the excuse for a good macho brawl, the crucial but essentially unimportant Hitchcockian McGuffin that moves the plot.

At any rate, and at long last, we are left with this: a universal myth, one which characteristically begins and often ends in an ideal place, and which is always populated by the same figures who always use similar magical tools and perform similar magical rites to get where they want to go; a myth which, although always the same, is manifested in different ways in different times and different places, even in different groups in the same time and place; a myth which, once it is divided in these ways, becomes further complicated with the addition of conflict, *archetypal* conflict, which itself always follows the same pattern. This myth appears in every aspect of conscious human life, on every level from the sublime to the much less so: that it appears in sport exactly as it appears in the familiar tales of the antique era should surprise no one.

PART TWO

THE
APPLICATION
OF THEORY
TO SPORT

Chapter 3

THE ARCHETYPES OF SPORT

Myth and the urge to heroize seem to be profoundly a part of man's nature and will persist no matter how strong the forces working against them.

—Ray B. Browne
(*Heroes of Popular Culture* 186)

It appears at first glance ludicrous to consider the hero of myth and the athlete-hero as analogous.... but the comparison is justified on two grounds. First...the sources [of the character of the athlete-hero] may be the same sources that spontaneously produce mythic symbols.... Second, the psychoanalytical approach to myth, adopted by Otto Rank, Joseph Campbell, and others, emphasizes that heroic myths are allegories of the process of maturation.

—Michael Oriard
(*Dreaming of Heroes* 36-37)

[A] large element of make-believe...is present in all sporting activity.... Make-believe does not enter in the same proportion into all sports, but it is present in a very appreciable degree in all.... [in] the scheme of life of the leisure class, [sports] afford a colorable pretense of purpose, even if the object assigned be only make-believe.

—Thorstein Veblen
(*The Theory of the Leisure Class* 256-59)

When Veblen uses the childish term "make-believe" to describe the willing suspension of disbelief that occurs in all games, he echoes Huizinga's suggestion that "playing" is central to myth-making, and he reinforces (like Oriard) the connection between the heroes created in sport and those made in more conventional venues.

Since Veblen's time our culture has grown more and more hospitable to non-traditional myths. Frazer would very likely agree that the steady inroads of science, by wearing out many of our creeds, have encouraged the formation of new, popular, or "vulgar" ones. One of the myths that has gained in power in modern times, partly for such reasons, is the one involving the "make-believe" of organized games: as Huizinga says, "ever since the last quarter of the 19th century games, in the guise of sport, have been taken more and more seriously" (197).

Technology and urbanization, themselves offshoots of science, seem to have played their parts as well; Frederick Cozens and Florence Stumpf suggest that the need for sports heroes and myths may have arisen after "the increasing impersonal quality of city life created a greater need for vicarious personal contacts and for humanized materials which would permit the illusion of sharing an emotional experience." Robert Higgs, denying that we live "in an antiheroic age," says:

> The sports world belies such assertions. Here the hero is alive and well. It is not a question of whether or not heroes are dead but rather what type of heroism is popular at any particular time in history. (137)

While Huizinga's theory that Veblen's "make-believe" creates some sort of myth makes very good sense, the other theorists I have discussed in the previous chapters are just as important, since they investigate the childish or primitive psyche that thinks up those games in the first place, nor is there any lack of application of their ideas to sport. When Oriard applied "the Jungian myth of psychic integration" to Malamud's *The Natural* more than a decade ago, he bluntly said that he didn't have to spend much time explaining the application of Jung to that novel, since "this material has been handled expertly by others" (214). And listen to Howard Slusher's reason for our need for heroes:

Man does not enjoy facing death. To maintain immortality
in the sporting hero is one way for each of us to keep our
association with the far-reaching past. In this way, we
each stay alive a little longer and our life is also that
much richer. (756)

That, of course, is precisely the motive for myth-making
suggested by Rank's third principle, as well as by R.D. Laing
and Ernest Becker. It is by no means an academic stretch to
emphasize the importance of the ideas of men like Jung and
Rank to any analysis of the psychic workings of sport and
our fascination with it.

A. The Archetypal Journey in Sport

If popular sports really are particular manifestations of
archetypal myths, they will also reflect the monomyth's
components; they will have narratives or "plots," archetypally
formulaic characters, tools, locations and conflicts. They do,
of course. To begin with sports "plot": I've said that the
archetypal narrative pattern consists of a journey toward
knowledge followed by a return to a "home" which has been
altered by that knowledge, and this sequence is central to
sport, too; as Allen Guttmann points out, "sports too have
their seasons, like primitive myths of eternal return" (178).
In fact, the mythical pattern that forms the basis for sport is
the same one found at the heart of two other forms of public
ceremony, drama and religion.

Noting the parallels between games and the theater,
Francis Keenan says sport, "like the drama, functions as a
mechanism for the celebration or enforcement of traditions of
race or group," adding that the appropriate verb for each
activity is "to play." Keenan points out that the theater and
the arena were often adjacent in ancient Greece, and goes on
to say that there is an "Aristotelian paradigm" to the sports
event, which event resembles tragedy in that it also
"symbolizes man's struggle with the inequities and paradoxes
of life," a symbolism made more cathartic because, although
the sport remains only a game, the action of sport, unlike
that of drama, "is real." Keenan's sports hero has the "will to
win" that will carry him past "adversity" to a "comeback,"

thus fulfilling the expulsion/quest/return pattern of the archetypal narrative (311-18). Later, Christian Messenger calls the figure described by Keenan the "Ritual Sports Hero," saying he is "an Adamic figure who seeks self-knowledge" (205).

When Don Calhoun comments on this argument, he claims Keenan hasn't gone far enough; for Calhoun, the power of sport is that it always illustrates Rank's third principle:

> Francis W. Keenan says, "The tragedy teaches us that for many men the ultimate achievement is defeat and that the highest level of performance, the most noble effort, may end in defeat." The agon is "an example of man's plight in an uncertain world. I think Keenan understates the point: the world is uncertain, true, but one thing is certain—for all people (not "many") all effort will (not "may") end in personal death. (301)

Sport is also archetypally close to religion. Keenan and Calhoun both refer to Aristotle and to the origin of sport in the classical era, and we should remember that in ancient Greece both drama and sport were functions of faith. Whether sport is or is not religion is less a matter of debate than one of semantics since in every scenario sport remains a myth. Michael Novak insists that sport is religion, and while Harry Edwards dismisses the idea of religiosity in the athlete's approach to the game, he is as convinced as anyone of the strong parallels between the myths of faith and those of games, noting that each has its creed, saints, gods, shrines, symbols, etc. (260-62).

In any event, it's obvious that the "plots" of both Greek drama and religious scripture follow the archetypal pattern of the monomyth, as glances at the Oresteia or the book of Job will attest—and, just as the athlete's mythical journey updates the trips taken by heroes of classical myth, so are the places he visits during that journey contemporary versions of archetypal stages.

B. Stages on the Journey

Some natural tears they dropped,
  but wiped them soon.
The world was all before them,
  where to choose
Their place of rest, and Providence
  their guide.
They, hand in hand, with wandering steps
  and slow,
Through Eden took their solitary way.

—John Milton
(*Paradise Lost* 11. 645-49)

There the young monks every day
After dinner go out to play;
There is no hawk or quail so swift,
Half as nimble or as deft,
As these monks in joyous mood,
Their long sleeves flying and their hood
Floating on the evening air
As they dance across the lawn.
When the abbot sees them flee,
Who more joyous is than he?
Till he summons them along,
Crying, "Time for even-song!"
But feisty monks absorbed in play
Romp over the hills and far away.

—Anonymous
(*Cockayne* 100)

I didn't weep at Mathewson's death.... it raised him beyond the heights he'd known in youth. He became legend.

—Eric Rolfe Greenberg
(*The Celebrant* 268)

Departure from Arcadia, arrival in Utopia and, finally, installation in Valhalla—or so every hero, and every athlete, always hopes. Of the three stages of the successful hero-journey, Arcadia is the least relevant; it is only the vestibule, the waiting area where the hero waits for his trip to begin; being essentially pre-heroic, it is also the only stage in which he remains on a level with the non-heroic. Once he has left Arcadia, the hero strives to avoid the Underworld in order to gain Utopia, a place in which he will be able to experience the perfection of happiness, a paradise greater than that from which he has been forced: Utopia is the ultimate earthly end of every hero's quest.

It is necessary to qualify the athletic Utopia as "earthly" because of the unavoidable separation, in sports myth, of the mythic and the biographical. Every athlete "dies" twice, once at the end of his mythic career, when he is no longer able to play, and once as a real individual; every athlete must leave his playing field before middle age has fully set in. As A.E. Housman ironically says, he's a "smart lad" if he dies young, thus sparing himself the pain of observing, as a real individual, his own mythic death. Athletes probably use the self-conscious third-person more than any other group of public figures. This is a little like the opera star who refers to her "instrument," instinctively aware that the talent belongs more to myth than reality. Jocks, like divas, are aware of their double lives, and their schizoid vacillation between first and third persons acknowledges the distinction between individual and fulfilled archetype.

The mythic life and the biological are separated in sport more than in any other area; musicians (even rock musicians, like the Rolling Stones' Mick Jagger and the Nearly Dead's Jerry Garcia) need not be affected by aging, and stage and movie stars can play "young" roles long after they themselves have grown old. In sport, however, this is never the case, and the delightful exceptions (Gordie Howe, George Blanda, Nolan Ryan) only prove the rule. The trauma of finding yourself mythically "dead" in your thirties takes its toll on all athletes, as can be seen in the recurrent pattern of old players (particularly boxers) who can't resist the lure of trying one more time. Even Sam Malone, the old Red Sox pitcher on the TV sitcom *Cheers*, once tried a Jim Bouton, Fernando Valenzuela-style comeback.

During his mythic "life" (his career), the athlete tries to reach the *earthly* Utopia which is associated with success in his quest—Wimbledon, the Boston Garden, Soldier Field, Yankee Stadium—and to stay there as long as he can. After his mythic "death," though, he is still alive as a real individual; now his effort will be to become a "legend," to enter Valhalla, the celestial paradise—the shrines for golf or hockey, Canton or Cooperstown, even the less formal legacy of an indestructible image, like those of George Gipp or Phar Lap. But if he is neither an active player (if he's mythically "dead") nor as yet accepted as one of the immortals, he may be in the worst place for an athlete: the Underworld.

The Underworld in sport is negative, not so much a place as an *absence* of place; just as the worst punishment in either Dante's hell or Milton's is the separation of the soul from God, so the fallen or stricken athlete's punishment is banishment from the game, removal of any chance he has at achieving first Utopia, then Valhalla. Achilles hated his hell because there was no fighting to do; Buck Weaver or Pascual Perez would understand, as would those tragically hurt, like Dennis Bird or Ron Turcotte, or those who, like Ernie Banks, just never wanted it to end.

The athlete whose mythical life is over and who has been condemned to the Underworld usually prays for (and often lives and lobbies for) the positive afterlife of Valhalla. The Underworld and Valhalla are important in sport myth because the athlete, unlike the conventional hero, has two extremely distinct lives, and because his life in myth and his life in the world of time seldom if ever merge. Even the old Lear dies "every inch a king," concluding both his myth and his biography at the same moment; the athlete never does, and the athlete can't, unless his biological life is tragically shortened.

To summarize: if the hero moves from the pastoral paradise of Arcadia to the earthly and perfected one of Utopia and finally to Valhalla, all the while side-stepping the dangers of the Underworld, he remains a hero; if he doesn't, he either becomes a fallen hero, a pariah (this is *his* fault), or a martyr (this is *not*). As we will see, sometimes the climate of the times (the temporal location of the myth) will play a large part in determining whether an individual athlete fills the "slot" of pariah or that of martyr.

Finally, let me add a few comments on the places where the athlete-heroes play. If a Utopian setting characteristically combines nature and architecture (which themselves reflect Dionysiac energy and Apollonian order), it's small wonder that stadia, particularly in baseball, are so important to players and fans alike. Philip Lowry (probably borrowing the term from Michael Novak) called ballparks "green cathedrals" and the name, reaching us where we archetypally live, has stuck.

Why do fans get so upset when an old arena is torn down, even though the one built to replace it is invariably more comfortable in every aspect? Why do we insist on real grass, not plastic, whenever we can get it? Why was Camden Yard built in the first place, if not in the pragmatic owners' confidence that, once they built it, the fans would come? In his analysis of Malamud, Oriard points out that Roy Hobbs, "the natural," is incompatible with the man-made city, and that this incompatibility is what makes him fail (217). In non-fictional sports myth, though, the confrontation of urban and bucolic characteristically results in an ideal blending.

Another explanation for the mythic pull of the sports stadium goes even deeper, and is suggested by Novak, who points out that "those oval stadiums and circular domes within which our three national liturgies are consummated are indeed feminine in their symbolism" (American 46). Is it possible that the building that houses the game is an echo of Neumann's "Great Container," a symbol of the great mother in both her nurturing and destructive aspects? More than possible, it's probable, at least for sports played in the fresh air.

If you dismiss this notion as outlandish, you must also reject Freud's position that the nave of a church is matric. I would even go so far as to suggest that every male athlete who appears in a stadium before an approving crowd is acting out the role of the son defeating the father and stealing the affection of the mother. But if that seems too much for you, we can at least say this: when we play our games on a measured and ordered portion of our natural earth (a "field," a "park," a "yard"), we are doing exactly what the Greeks did when they built their amphitheaters and running tracks outdoors, ordering nature further by choosing each location carefully.

Despite all this, however, it's very obvious that all sporting venues do not combine the structural and the organic: some sports, such as cross-country skiing or running, are entirely pastoral, while others, such as boxing, hockey, and basketball, are normally played in an entirely architectural setting, albeit one that frequently and wistfully is called a "garden." It may be possible to say that these exceptions prove the rule, since the three games just mentioned all originated outdoors. However, it could also explain why outdoor sports such as baseball, football, rugby, cricket, and soccer tend to be more important to fans around the world than most of their roofed and housed counterparts.

C. The Archetypal Sports Figures

The athlete incorporates "*a mythical ideal.*" Is he, then, a Hercules or Prometheus, or sometimes even a Narcissus? The ideal of cultural achievement beyond the requirements of survival and everyday affairs somehow makes man the culturally creative, spiritual, intellectual, and symbolic being he is....The athlete can be interpreted as representing the "myth," instantiating a sort of "mythical" figure of a Herculean-Promethean kind; he is a *cultural god.*

—Hans Lenk
("Herculean 'Myth' Aspects of Athletics" 441)

Being an active player is like living in the select circle of the gods.

—Michael Novak
(*The Joy of Sports* 132)

My songs, lords of the lyre,
Which of the gods, what hero, what mortal
    shall we celebrate?

—Pindar
second Olympiad

As I've said, modern sporting heroes and gods are created in the same way heroes and gods were created in the ancient world, and by now contemporary writers have begun to note this reflexively, as when Oriard comments that "the star athlete may be a diminished hero, but he is our only link to the Adonises and Galahads of the past" (220). As I think this habit of referring to the manifestations of archetypal categories by reference to established myth is not only natural but accurate, I will not make much reference to the categories of sports hero established by recent scholars such as Orrin Klapp and Garry Smith; instead, I'll go directly to the ancient source, and try to show how modern athletes are, just as Oriard says, exactly the same kinds of mythic figures as were their pre-historic forbears.

When personal archetypes like mine are set up as "slots" and we begin to look around for real individuals to "fill" them, there is a real danger that the process will become subjective, inviting disagreement between those who can't decide which archetype a particular athlete represents. Unfortunately, there is no clear way to skirt this problem, which has confronted everyone who has assigned mythic roles to sports heroes. Tristram Coffin, for example, calls Cobb a crafty trickster, and it would be my own choice to follow his lead, but might not a man who charged through his game like Cobb also be a productive Dionysiac? Sadly, these are not the sort of disagreements that can be settled at two in the morning in your favorite tavern simply by asking the barkeep to pass over the *Baseball Encyclopedia*. Nonetheless, somebody's got to do this tough job, and you will find my own suggestions for individuals who have been made into types in the pages that follow.

I should point out at the start that I name fewer females than males for the obvious reason that sport is sexist, very largely and sometimes exclusively (as in major and minor league baseball) male. If I give women in sport less than equal time it is only because that's how society has treated them; as Robert Higgs says, "the fact that 'the golden people' of [sport's] 'golden age' were all white males with one or two exceptions, does not mean that the law would not work for others, but merely that others have not had the opportunity to try it for themselves" (140). There is even the possibility that sexism in sport, like the myth-making faculty itself, extends all the way back on the evolutionary scale to early or even pre-humans. Some anthropologists believe that the earliest hunters fell into two separate categories, being either sensible "providers" or macho "show-offs," and that the latter (always male) may have been the first to organize and play competitive games.

In making my categories, I've decided that no individual athletes, not even the Babes, Ruth and Didrickson, can rise to the level of "great father" and "great mother," since those huge figures contain all the qualities of the figures beneath them, and in a sense *lose* their archetypal definition and integrity by being *too* all-inclusive. Certainly fans and writers often describe their heroes using the general and undifferentiated terms "god" (Ruth) and "goddess" (Suzanne Lenglen), but even then there is further definition: both Ruth and the possibly self-destructive and certainly short-lived Lenglen were probably primarily Dionysiacs. When Paul Gallico talks about the Dempsey congregation, he says only that a god is being adored:

> The cult of Dempsey-worshippers was a public love and idolatry that transcended anything ever known in the ring and perhaps, for that matter, in any sport. (14)

Still, is there any doubt that a man nicknamed the "Mauler" is a Dionysiac figure? If there is, all you need to do is imagine him across the ring from his most famous opponent. Gene Tunney, an avid reader of the classics, was an Apollonian if there ever was one.

Both Tunney and Dempsey, of course, were very good at what they did, and hence productive; although Dempsey was beaten, he remains secure in Valhalla, arguably the most famous fighter ever (he even had a species of aggressive fish named after him), and Tunney retired undefeated. Can we find examples of the other archetypes if we look further in boxing?

Certainly. If Tunney, the smart boxer, was a traditional Apollonian sage, Muhammad Ali and Archie Moore were both tricksters, and any fighter who was fooled when Moore pretended to be groggy or who was roped into dopiness by Ali was a failed Apollonian, or a fool. And misdirected or destructive Dionysiacs, of course, abound in what ring announcer Harry Balogh once called "the annals of fistiana"; the ring is littered with them. As great as he was, you could argue that Jack Johnson was one; Mike Tyson certainly is. As far as Dionysiac failures, men just not strong enough to win, most are not very memorable because they lost; the chief exceptions are the great fighters who simply met greater ones, like Joe Frazier losing to Ali in Manila or Joe Louis when he fought Marciano.

Now let me turn to the six variants of these six main archetypes:

Martyrs and Pariahs

Once again, a martyr is a hero whose mythic life (his life as an athlete) is cut short in its prime, and the examples here, being matters of fact, are indisputable. In baseball, Lou Gehrig; in football, Ernie Davis; in thoroughbred racing, Ron Turcotte; in boxing, Benny "Kid" Paret. The sub-category of athletes stricken after their careers were over, or very nearly so, is an interesting one (think of Christy Mathewson, Willie Shoemaker, Arthur Ashe, and even Roberto Clemente), since only those whose lives "on the outside" were admirable seem included. When Sonny Liston died, for example, few mourned, because he was viewed as unsavory in real life: the public felt he had probably brought it on himself in some shady way, despite substantial evidence suggesting he was the innocent victim of a murder.

The pariah, justly denied his mythic life by some higher power, is always someone who has betrayed the code of the game. Sometimes the code is very much a local and cultural one, like the wearing of frilly shorts at Wimbledon or the expulsion of Eleanor Holm from the 1936 Olympic team after she was caught drinking champagne with three sports writers; more often it is the universal code, the treason of every game, cheating. The jockey who reins in his horse, the fighter who takes a dive, the forward who shaves points, the outfielder who intentionally throws to the wrong base—once caught, they become pariahs and are relegated to the Underworld.

Youth and Age

An athlete is necessarily neither a child nor old; since he needs a healthy and mature body for his mythic success, he can be neither Mozart nor Nestor (the exceptions, batboys or mascots and managers like Connie Mack, are not players). As a result, any deviation from the athlete's "normal" age is very noticeable. We notice players who are either younger or older than the expected norm, and we react to them differently, usually by according them more sympathy.

The nature of our reaction may depend to an extent upon whether the athlete is Apollonian or Dionysiac. Apollonian figures, of course, are associated with the spirit or the mind, Dionysiacs with the body or physical energy; all of us are aware that the body slowly decays, just as we all know that the mind slowly, incrementally adds to its store of knowledge. In Yeats' terms, we expect the body to become more and more tattered, while the soul sings louder and louder.

As a result of these natural facts, the older the Dionysiac athlete gets, the more sympathy we tend to feel and the more we admire his triumphs, since triumphs at his age are unexpected; conversely, we tend to admire a young Apollonian who is unusually mature or savvy for his age, since he's supposed to be a greenhorn, a fool, a silly "rook." An example of the latter might be tennis star Pete Sampras, but there are many more examples of the former, since we seem particularly fond of the jock-in-decline who turns in one last performance. I've already mentioned Howe, Blanda, and Ryan; think also of Jimmy Connors, Jack Nicklaus, of Babe Ruth's three homers in one game in his last year, or of Jersey Joe Walcott. Boxing, in fact, seems particularly fertile in providing us with over-the-hill athletes to cheer (or pray) for; even in fiction, the sentimentalized old fighter is a familiar fixture, as in Jack London's "A Piece of Steak" or Hemingway's "The Battler." Nonetheless, this is not an absolute rule; we can also sympathize with the old athlete whose mind (rather than his body) is in decline, just as we can feel sorry that Shakespeare's mental choir is no longer filled with the song of sweet birds, and we can delight in the achievements of the physically precocious (rather than the mental); as I've said, we love the story of David in the Bible.

Role-Changing or Mask-Wearing

Any of the personal archetypes can appear to be something else, can put on a costume or disguise, can wear a mask. For example, it is not uncommon for a player to *pretend* he is either a loser or a fool. If a fighter (Ali, Moore) pretends he is hurt in order to get his opponent to drop his guard, he is pretending to be a Dionysiac failure, or physical loser; if a player pretends to make a mistake (Germany Schaefer running the bases clockwise) in order to steal a run, he is pretending to be an Apollonian failure, or fool. In both of these cases, however, the truth is soon disclosed; once Ali and Moore win their fights, they can't be considered losers, and once that run scores, Schaefer is seen as not silly but clever. In these cases, the athletes are quickly unmasked, and they then return to their real category, which of course is that of the trickster.

There are, however, athletes who wear masks for their entire mythic lives. Babe Ruth comes to mind. Although Ruth had a great deal of the dissolute and destructive Dionysiac in him, he always wore the mask of the constructive one, and even now that's how he's remembered—that's his role in Valhalla. Was Mathewson the saint he was supposed to be, or did he have elements of the trickster? After all, he's supposed to have participated in a "white lie" after the Merkle boner, when McGraw is said to have brought him to the Polo Grounds at night to watch Fred Merkle step on second base. After that, the story goes, Matty could tell the umps, honestly, that Merkle had touched second base, and that he had seen him do it.

And Lou Gehrig—didn't he cheat on his wife? Or George Gipp: wasn't he much more at home in bars and pool halls than in the chapel at South Bend? The most common archetypal mask is that worn by the all-too-human (and therefore physical) Dionysiac who pretends to be much holier (that is, more spiritual) and Apollonian than thou. Dwight

Gooden, an admitted drug abuser who was recently accused of sexual assault, remains an absolutely upright citizen for most of us, whatever the facts; we wouldn't have it any other way.

It's also common for pussycat Apollonians to pretend they are savage and out-of-control Dionysiacs, lambs turned tiger, but for whatever reason this never seems to work, and the boxers glaring at each other at the weigh-in or during the ref's instructions usually look no more sincere to us than WWF wrestlers.

Although masks are commonly worn by athletes, it's less usual for them to change their archetypal spots. While many if not most athletes represent a plural number of archetypes, they normally do not abandon one for another: Jack Dempsey, for example, could not have become an Apollonian had his mythic life depended on it. Nonetheless, there are sufficient examples of this happening to make it necessary to mention it. When the aging fast-ball pitcher is forced to learn how to throw "junk" in order to keep his career alive, for example, he has moved from the Dionysiac side of the ledger to the more cerebral Apollonian one (crafty division). On the other side of the coin, Apollonians are sometimes converted to the Dionysiac faith. This may be what happened in those years when Musial hit for distance or, more recently, when super-middleweight Michael Nunn dramatically turned from a defensive fighter into a knockout puncher; and, although *The Quiet Man* is fiction, Nunn's transformation parallels that of John Wayne's Trooper Thorn in that film.

As is the case in more conventional myth, when an athlete changes roles, we often see him in an ethical light: he is either "saved," like Magdalene, or he "falls," like Lucifer. In this category the ethical judgment is a matter of the location (in place, time and cultural group) of the athlete. As we'll see, heroes in one location can be goats in another. In other words, although the pattern I'm about to discuss is universal, the particular standards of its location will determine which individuals are chosen to "fill" it. This is why many people thought of Cassius Clay as a "fallen" hero just after he became Ali and was indicted for dodging the draft, and also why that view of Ali was reversed very quickly, once the times and their standards changed.

There is a recent example of this process at work in the cases and coverage of Mike Tyson and Magic Johnson. Tyson was convicted of rape; Johnson admitted he'd contracted the HIV virus through heterosexual promiscuity. How would they be judged by their culture, their time, and their place?

The results were mixed, indicating another philosophical division within the community. *The New Yorker* talked about Johnson's "generosity of spirit" (25 Nov. 1991: 40). Robert Lipsyte wished that judging the two men could be as simple as saying that Tyson was evil and Johnson was good, and then went on to add, "maybe it is" that simple (*New York Times*, 29 Dec. 1991). But Dave Anderson, also writing for the *Times*, said that Johnson and Tyson should be equally censured, that Magic was nobody's hero, that he had no "sense of sexual morality," even suggesting that the Deity himself disapproved of Magic's sexuality. After quoting Johnson's claim that "Everything I've done, He's directed me," Anderson sardonically added, "Not quite everything, as Magic Johnson knows too well now" (14 Nov. 1991).

When he wrote that column, Anderson placed himself firmly in the tradition of the "puritan heritage" of which we hear so much, and which has always been a part of the American ethos. Take Shoeless Joe Jackson. Archetypally, he moves from a selfless team player to a crafty trickster. So far, this is not an ethical problem; it's only when you realize that he used his craft *selfishly*, to betray a trust, that the ethics of the situation emerge. In fact, it is even more complicated than this, since in one sense Jackson remained a selfless "team player," at least for some of his peers, since he kept their secret. Nonetheless, the climate in which Jackson lived played a large part in creating his myth, exaggerating the extent of his guilt enormously, as I'll try to show later on.

There are fewer examples of individuals who have abandoned their sinful ways to become more saintly. On the Black Sox, we have the untainted Dickie Kerr, Eddie Collins and (possibly) Buck Weaver, but they were never prodigal, they just were either unaware of or refused temptation. If we turn again to Hollywood, though, we can find numerous examples, like John Garfield's boxer in *Body and Soul* or Robert Ryan's in *The Set-Up*, men who agree to take a dive but then decide not to. An Apollonian choice, surely, as any conscious choice must be; the reaction of the cheated mobster may be expected to be lethal, but at least the pug's spirit or *soul* will survive the loss of his Dionysiac body. As Garfield says to a menacing hood at the end of his movie, "What are you gonna do, kill me? *Everybody* dies."

Finally, don't forget that an individual may fall or rise on the purely Dionysiac level, too. There is little that's ethical in that process, however, unless you consider duty to self. The destructive and undirected Dionysiac can get his life together, as witness the numerous contemporary examples of drug-users who are now clean (Steve Howe, Lawrence Taylor); tragically, the process is often reversed, and great athletes can sacrifice their mythic lives (Hack Wilson, Pascual Perez) and sometimes even their biographical ones (Pelle Lindstrom, Len Bias, Ed Delahanty) in moving from orderly to chaotic Dionysiac energy.

D. Archetypal Sports Tools

The archetypal tools of myth, as I've said, may be either physical (in which case they are usually magical) or conceptual (like the good luck ritual or the jinx). They are also very often fundamentally (or archetypally) symbolic, as can certainly be seen in the many ball-and-stick games which combine phallic and matric elements. While I would like to reserve the bulk of my remarks about archetypal tools for my discussion of baseball, it should be obvious that, which the exception of events involving racing, there is hardly a major sport that does not have this ball-and-stick basis, with its sexual undertones, as a pattern. Let me list a few such sports, including the "stick," the "ball," and the "goal" the ball must reach:

Sport	Stick	Ball	Goal
1. baseball	bat	baseball	stands
2. football	arm, leg	football	end zone, goal posts
3. basketball	arm	basketball	net
4. hockey	stick	puck	net
5. soccer	leg	soccer ball	net
6. rugby	arm, leg	rugby ball	goal posts
7. lacrosse	stick w/ net	ball	net
8. tennis	racket w/ net	tennis ball	"in" zone
9. polo	mallet	ball	goal posts
10. golf	club	golf ball	hole
11. pool	cue	pool ball	pocket
12. darts	arm	dart	dart board

I don't think we need a therapist to analyze this pattern for us, or to suggest some subliminal reasons why some sports may be so popular.

Regarding specific physical tools, it's well known that individual players will insist on using their pet implements, partly because they feel they are better tools, but it's equally well known that athletes are not above superstition, and they they will go to great and remarkable lengths to propitiate their household gods. Thus, in addition to a favorite lance (bat, racket, golf club, pool cue), the hero may carry an amulet to ward off bad luck or a talisman to bring good, or perform a lucky ritual or recite a magical incantation to ensure the proper outcome. Finally, his team may enlist the aid of a palladium, that magical device which protects the entire group. The most common palladium in sport is probably one which is unique, a little mystical in itself, because it's intangible and abstract: the home-court advantage.

Chapter 4

LOCALIZED SPORTS ARCHETYPES

A. *Place, Time and Cultural Group*

All of these archetypes—plots, persons, places, and tools—are colored by their location, whether that setting is in place (regional), time (temporal), or socio-economic group (cultural). Baseball is not played today as it was in the previous century, nor is it played in this country as it is in Japan; cock and bull fighting are as popular in some cultures as they are deplored in others.

Place: Regions

Contrasting the sports fiction of the United States with that of Great Britain, Oriard finds a general cultural pattern in that "winning is unimportant" for the British, whereas here it's as revered as Vince Lombardi. Differences in the myth's location will determine which of the archetypes is most admired. If we accept Oriard's conclusion, for example, a trickster who helped win a game through craft would be admired stateside, but suspected or even criticized in England. Novak goes so far as to say that the archetype a culture most admires defines that culture better than anything the culture might consciously reveal:

> The type of character celebrated, more likely than not, reveals the unconscious needs of the civilization— extols the very qualities that more highly conscious formulations are likely to deny. (Joy 29)

Time: Eras

A sport and its myth must be located in time as well as in place. Lipsky points out that the athlete's era affects his image when he claims "we can learn a great deal about the values that are taking hold within ordinary lives and mass

57

consciousness by looking at who rises as an athletic hero at a particular time (107)," and Cozens and Stumpf, comparing the climate of a given historical period to its athletic heroes, add that "the thoughtful reader can scarcely escape the conclusion that these are not *entirely* unrelated (126)." They are very much related, of course, as Oriard points out in impressive detail in his survey of the changes in our culture over the past century or so, *Sporting With the Gods.*

Several others (Garry Smith, Richard Lipsky, Gerard O'Connor) provide sketches of this history: O'Connor says the Apollonian Hobey Baker was the most admired sports figure of his time (that of the First World War), suggesting his Adonic martyrdom in that war made him his era's perfect god (88), though he is surely mistaken when he says Baker's was the first archetypal image to combine symbolism and charisma with great skill: the first U.S. athlete to do that was also the greatest popular hero of any kind in his era, John L. Sullivan. Smith acknowledges this in naming Sullivan first on his list of sports heroes of the late nineteenth century, but, curiously, he lumps him with James J. Corbett, a very dissimilar figure who was admired for entirely different reasons. In fact, the Dionysiac Sullivan was the ideal hero for the 1880s, while Corbett represented that part of an increasingly sophisticated American culture which had taken a back seat to the rough ethos of the frontiersman in the 1880s, but which was shortly going to move into and then become the mainstream. The Sullivan-Corbett fight is a fine illustration of how myth is located, and I'll discuss it later in some detail.

Cultural Groups

When Corbett beat Sullivan, there may have been nostalgia, but there was no bickering. The country, which could read the symbolism, knew the times had begun to change. But the conflict between different cultures which often co-exist within the same region is not always just a question of the new replacing the old; it can be a question of evenly matched hostile camps, fighting for the same space during the same time. Politically, that's a description of our Civil War; socially and philosophically, it describes many periods of American history, most recently the sixties. In this confrontational decade, says O'Connor, the biggest sports hero was the iconoclastic and pleasure-seeking Joe Namath (95), and Smith, reminding us that "the sports hero is an accurate barometer of the times," would probably agree, especially since he adds that sixties athletes, "instead of conforming, wanted to express their individuality" (115). Lipsky's analysis shows clearly that these were times of conflict, not growth:

> The turmoil of the 1960s saw the breakdown of consensus in American society. The rise of sports heroes with divergent appeals reflected this breakdown. Who one rooted for began to be determined by the athlete's political views and life-style. The politicization of athletes added to the possibilities for hero worship and villainy. (117)

In fact, it is hard not to think of Ali's fights against Foreman or the flag-waving Frazier as proof of Lipsky's pudding. And, even though it would not happen until after Reagan became President, the 1984 world series provided another good example of cultural confrontation within the same nation, at least, although the regions were very different. In wealthy, conservative San Diego, the fans in the stands waved little American flags; in poor, blue-collar Detroit, they tore the place apart.

While there are obviously many more examples of sport myth set in regional, temporal, and cultural locales, at least one more should be mentioned, the second Louis-Schmeling fight. This memorable match, one of Louis' greatest, was unique in combining a regional context with a cultural one. The regional locations, Nazi Germany and the United States, could hardly have been more culturally different, at least in the public's perception, and the cultural difference between the two men, being racial, was even more obvious. Anthony Edmonds has written a lengthy analysis of this fight's social and symbolic significance, and so no more need be said here, other than that Louis won a victory for both the country and its blacks. Democracy defeated Fascism; a (nominally) free black man defeated a member of the supposed master race.

In reality, of course, these simple distinctions were more complex; Schmeling was neither much of a racist nor much of a Nazi, and a democratic country that still both encouraged and legislated the same racism Louis was supposedly attacking could hardly be called Athenian. Again, however, we have to remember that we're dealing with myth and archetype, not with the individuals who make real history; in 1938, Joe Louis was the perfect hero, Max Schmeling, the perfect villain. This brings us to the general question of heroes and villains, winners and losers, and I'd like to turn to that now.

B. The Agon in Sport

Sports...afford an exercise for dexterity and for the emulative ferocity and astuteness characteristic of predatory life.... The immediate and unreflected purposefulness of sports, in the way of expression of dominance, will measurably satisfy [the individual's] instinct of workmanship. This is especially true if his dominant impulses are the unreflecting emulative propensities of the predacious temperament....

Football is the particular game which will probably first occur to anyone in this community when the question of the serviceability of athletic games is raised.... It has been said, not inaptly, that the relation of football to physical culture is much the same as that of the bullfight to agriculture. Serviceability for these institutions requires sedulous training or breeding. The material used, whether brute or human, is subjected to careful selection and discipline, in order to secure and accentuate certain aptitudes and propensities...which tend to obsolescence under domestication.... The result is a one-sided return to barbarism or to the *feroe natura*—a rehabilitation and accentuation of those ferine traits which make for damage and desolation.... The culture bestowed in football gives a product of exotic ferocity and cunning....

Ferocity and cunning are of no use to the community except in its hostile dealings with other communities.

As it finds expression in the life of the barbarian, prowess manifests itself in two main directions—force and fraud. In varying degrees these two forms of expression are similarly present in modern warfare, in the pecuniary occupations, and in sports and games. Both lines of aptitudes are cultivated and strengthened by the life of sport....

The gifts and exploits of Ulysses are scarcely second to those of Achilles, either in their substantial furtherance of the game or in the eclat which they give the astute sporting man among his associates.

—Thorstein Veblen
(*The Theory of the Leisure Class* 260-62, 273-74)

If we take offense at Veblen's killjoy and supercilious attitude toward our games (is he *really* proposing that linebackers should be bred, like Miura bulls?), we should also take comfort in the fact that he is a truly awful writer of prose. Nonetheless, you'll note that his ideas are a good deal more palatable and persuasive than his style. Essentially, Veblen argues that sport is predatory behavior, symbolic or "safe" combat, and that it is characterized by two main thrusts: *force* (associated with Achilles) and *fraud* (associated with Ulysses). Games are agonistic; this necessarily means that, while they are being played, players become either "theirs" or "ours." The fraud of Ulysses and the force of Achilles are no longer restricted to a single archetypal pantheon; now they are turned against an opponent. As Novak points out, agon (the opposition of players or teams) requires location: "a team is not only assembled in one place; it also represents a place," he says (143), and Guttmann adds this:

Representational sport can diminish as well as increase a sense of community. Psychologists who testify to the enhancement of school spirit after "our" team has thrashed "them" have also noticed a tendency to doff the totemistic sweatshirt when the team falters in defeat. Representational sport depresses the vicarious losers and loosens the bonds of community. Partisans of the defeated side have been known to bicker among themselves over the causes of the defeat. (183)

Now a whole new set of archetypes, the agonistic, is created, although as I've said, the agonistic "slots" and the personal ones are not mutually exclusive. The new archetypes simply assign a universal function to the old ones, an active role; while the old ones were essentially static, the new are kinetic. The figural archetypes described what the athletes are; the agonistic ones show what they do.

Any sports contest must contain some of the six agonistic archetypes, and many will contain all of them; they are, you'll remember, HERO, HELPER, GOAL, RECEIVER, VILLAIN and JUDGE. Whenever Joe Montana completed a pass to Jerry Rice, he was the Hero, Rice was the Helper, the six points constituted the Goal, the team was the Receiver, and the opposing team's defense was the Villain. Obviously, the refs acted as Judge. As always, assignment of these categories to individuals can be somewhat arbitrary; while most observers would probably agree with the above analysis of that great Forty-Niners offense, Jerry Rice would undoubtedly say that he was Souriau's "hero" and that Montana was his "helper." In all this, a few general rules may be useful:

1. To have "safe combat," you must have more than one combatant; fairly viewed, this only means two or more agonists, but once the observer is associated with one "side" or the other, your side turns into the *protagonist*, the other(s) into the *antagonist(s)*.

2. Once the pantheon of personal archetypes has split into "sides," each new agonistic group will have the same archetypal pattern, that of the original pantheon.

3. Agonists must be associated with location. While it is unusual when this location is temporal, it sometimes happens, as when Corbett knocks out Sullivan. The most common agon involves two regional locations (East vs. West in the Olympics, Manchester vs. Leeds in British soccer), although agons can also be cultural (Jack Johnson vs. Jess Willard, Bobby Riggs vs. Billie Jean King).

And now I would like to take a more specific look at how this system applies to baseball.

PART THREE

THE
APPLICATION
OF THEORY
TO BASEBALL

Chapter 5

DISCLAIMER

Prince Albert's passion for baseball was a royal scandal. Rumor had it that the Prince was itching to throw out the first ball, an honor historically reserved for the President. So baseball-besotted was the Prince, went the rumor, that he had let it be known he would settle for throwing out the second ball.

Queen Victoria were often irritated by the Prince's un-English tastes, but this baseball passion had begun to get under her skins. When she first told Albert it would disgrace the Crown for him to throw out the second ball, a terrible row ensued.

Now this baseball nuisance had to be dealt with. Just this morning a leading newspaper had asked if she objected to its publishing a column by the prince on the spiritual essence of baseball.

As usual, she were not amused and told Prince Albert she weren't, while holding his column at arm's length. She knew what he was up to, all right. By filling op-ed pages with ridiculous gush about baseball's balletic beauty and symbolic meaning for constitutional monarchy, as well as its mythological significance, Albert thought he could get himself invited to throw out the second ball.

"We shall give it to you straight from the shoulders," she said. "We have read your column and commanded its suppression on artistic grounds: to wit, its Philistine attempt to perpetuate the absurd notion that baseball is a metaphor. Our patience is exhausted with journalistic hacks waxing lyrical about baseball being a metaphor. We should be humiliated were our dear Albert to be exposed as one of them."

—the late Queen in conversation with
her consort, as recorded by Russell Baker

65

We (that's the *journalistic* we, son) are fully aware of the tendency of many contemporary writers to oversolemnize baseball; to paraphrase Sam Johnson, they may think they write like Angells, but they sound like ordinary (and pretentious) men. We would therefore like to say in our defense that the theories advanced herein in no way suggest that baseball really is a celestial and corny cornfield in which lost players may find their salvation, or that it really is an edenic and timeless (and therefore deathless) island in the flawed world. In fact, being New Yorkers, we even have some trouble with the notion that heaven and Iowa are the same place. And so what follows is an attempt, cold-eyed and hard-headed (we hope), to show why Americans who follow baseball persist in feeling such desperate yearnings for people and places too good (or bad) to be true. Throughout, in other words, we have tried, very hard, not to be gushy.

Chapter 6

ORIGINS OF THE BASEBALL MYTH

We are standing here in a pantheon. We are in the presence of our simple, smiling gods.

—Christopher Lehmann-Haupt
(reviewing Roger Angell's *Season Ticket*)

Baseball is, in fact, a vital source of myth in a nearly mythless country.

—Michael Oriard
(*Dreaming of Heroes* 212)

Again, scholars of our species trace the playing of games far, far back in human history, some even suggesting that play precedes language. We know that foot races took place long before the Greek Olympics, in Egypt, at about 3000 B.C., at the Festival of Sed. Boxing may have surfaced in the Minoan Dodecanese about a millennium later, and it has been reasonably argued that the first sport ever, its date of origin too far back to have been recorded, was spear-throwing. If that is true, then the first human sport at least involved a stick, and was possibly (if a target was used) the progenitor of all ball-and-stick games.

Baseball, of course, is a ball-and-stick game. Consider its archetypal quality: baseball is based on the pattern of pursuit-and-capture; it's a variation on the simplest and most primeval child's game, tag. In tag, if the tagger can manage to touch the taggee, the victim is "it"; in baseball, if the fielder can touch the runner with the ball, the runner is "out." Further, because a stick is used, there are a couple of more adult patterns to baseball. First, that of one of pursuit-and-*conquer*, in which the child becomes a young man, and tag becomes the hunt; second, the erotic pattern.

Comparative mythology in its search for cognates has found an important parallel to ball-and-stick play in the many tales involving the Lance and the Cup. The hero of such a tale bears a lance, and usually seeks a cup; as Jessie Weston points out, these two elements are undisguisedly sexual. I would agree with Ms. Weston and contend that ball-and-stick games are the most phallic we have, since, while the Grail is only sought, the stick-wielder actually strikes the ball, the cup's spherical relative. But I would also argue that the action of the thrower is just as phallic as that of the player with the stick. The thrower's object is to throw the ball on a line like a javelin so that it gets past the batter, ending in a grail-like glove. This suggests that in baseball, despite the convention of thinking of the team in the field as warding off an aggressor and the team that's "up" as being on the phallic attack, *both* of the activities central to ball-and-stick games are aggressively sexual; don't forget that, in Montréal, a baseball pitcher is called a *lanceur*. Zeus himself, who hurls narrow, stick-like thunderbolts, can represent both striker and thrower, and this may be why Ruth, revered both as a pitcher and as a hitter, is baseball's greatest Olympian god. In all of this it's easy to see the fascinating ambivalence of ball-and-stick games: in baseball, while the batter is trying to "hit one out of the park," he is also doing his best to "guard the plate" so that he may "stay alive"; while the pitcher is trying to "strike the batter out," possibly by first "knocking him down," he may also be "preserving the lead" and "saving the game." One of the most characteristic qualities of baseball is that offense and defense are so homogeneously combined.

Ball-and-stick games are obviously firmly connected to our deepest and most Jungian portions. Think of the opening scene of Stanley Kubrick's film *2001*, in which an ape swings a thigh-bone: ball-and-stick games could seriously be neanderthal in origin, and they might go back even further. Still, the gradual growth of American baseball can be traced to games played earlier in Great Britain, and if we can't go all the way back to the "ur"-game, we can at least go part way. Let me give you a chronological overview of ball-and-stick games as they developed in Britain and

America from the medieval period down to the time of plastic grass:

ca. 500 A.D.—Anglo-Saxon Ball-Play, Northumbria. Nothing is known of the game, in which, it's said, St. Cuthbert himself indulged. It may have had harsh rules, since Cuthbert was eventually beheaded.

ca. 1200 A.D.—Stool Ball. The player either sits on a stool and hits a thrown ball with his hand, or stands in front of the stool and swats the thrown ball with a stick. In the second form, this is the source of baseball, especially since more stools are soon used, since their number eventually reaches four, since their function is identical to that of baseball's base, and since after a while they are actually called "bases."

ca. 1300 A.D.—Camp Ball, played until the eighteenth century in Norfolk, Suffolk, and Sussex. A sort of rugby with a cricket-sized ball. The player could use his hands, but not his feet; the ball could be struck or thrown, but not handed, from player to player, although it had to be carried by one player across the goal line, when that player's team would "win the notch or snotch."

—Kicking Camp Ball. Substitute a football for the cricket ball. In this game, the foot is surrogate stick.

—Savage Camp Ball. When you wear *shoes* while you're doing the kicking. In the reign of Edward II, there was an especially fierce match of Savage Camp at Shouldham in Norfolk. A canon coincidentally named William de Spalding ran into a layman during some spirited action, and the layman was fatally impaled upon the good canon's knife. A tragic accident, surely. Canon de Spalding was suspended, but after he applied to the Vatican he was reinstated.

ca. 1500 A.D.—Cricket, according to the modern school of thought. There is a real possibility that cricket was born in a specific pub in Hambledon, Wiltshire, in the United Kingdom. This pub, which is now called the Bat and Ball, still stands, and may be visited by those academics anxious for thorough research.

ca. 1800 A.D.—Round Ball, or Rounders, the form of stool ball which is next on the evolutionary scale; it was imported to the U.S. as early as 1820. The most important differences between rounders and baseball were that all batters on a side had to be put out before an inning was over, you could hit a runner with the ball to make an out, and you could also make an out by dropping the ball into a small hole.

1845 A.D.—The earliest baseball games are played in Hoboken, New Jersey, in a public park named Elysian Fields.

The above will correctly suggest that the rules of ball-and-stick games changed slowly, and I would add that the changes aren't very significant. What these games have in common—their deep psychic appeal—is much more important.

Now, having sketched its growth from within the ball-and-stick category, I'd like to turn to the patterns of baseball itself.

Chapter 7

THE ARCHETYPES OF BASEBALL

Is it too harsh to say that most of baseball history is
myth? Hardly.

—Peter C. Bjarkman
("Bums' Lit" 55)

A. *The Journey*
The trip taken by the baseball hero is no different from
that of any other mythic figure: he begins naively in an
Arcadia, grows into wisdom and finally, through that
wisdom, achieves Utopia. Along the way, he must avoid the
Underworld. After his heroic time and life are up, he will
hope to be received into Valhalla.

All of this happens in the hero's mythic life, not at all in
his real or biological one, and it happens exclusively to his
mythic persona, to the figure created by fans and reporters,
that figure which is often referred to in the third person by
the player himself. The climax of the mythical hero's journey
is his demonstration of knowledge. Just as the ancient hero
had to answer difficult questions or solve impossible riddles
in order to achieve heroic stature—to create himself—so the
ballplayer must learn. The rookie who fails to understand
the fundamentals will have trouble making it on McGraw's
team, or Earl Weaver's; the fast-ball pitcher who can't master
a curve will be "sent down," no matter how hard he throws;
had the extremely wild young Sandy Koufax never learned
to slow his pace, he never would have found his control, and
he never would have crossed this mythical bridge.

B. *The Stages*
The story of Mel Ott is a good illustration of the
archetypal stages along the baseball hero's mythic journey.
He begins in the innocent Arcadia of Gretna, Louisiana, a

kid of 15 who breaks down and cries when told he's too young to play for a local team; at 16, green as they come, he travels alone and terrified on a train to New York City, where he gets his first look at his Utopian goal, the Polo Grounds, but he doesn't fully enter that Utopia until he has learned a great deal; then he plays his first full season, at age 19. He leaves Utopia at 39, shortly thereafter entering the Valhalla at Cooperstown at the age of 41.

This is the complete biography of the mythic Mel Ott, and it is over in early middle age (the sad fact that Ott the individual also died young is irrelevant here). Ott was lucky enough to escape the Underworld, that place where the mythic hero is denied his function, where, through injury or banishment, he can no longer play his game (the minors should be considered a kind of limbo, not so bad as the Underworld but certainly not Utopia).

Here I would like to emphasize that the Utopian ballpark or "cathedral" does more than combine Dionysiac and Apollonian, anima and animus, as any Utopia must. First, it bears a surprising resemblance to Jung's mandala, the circle within the square. That this is only a coincidence based on the most convenient architectural design (a circle of seats within a square city block) is not relevant to the mythic pull such buildings will always have on the people who enter them.

Next, we must not forget that every ballpark is matric, Neumann's "great round" or "great container." As such, it is the only vestige of the Great Mother in the myth of baseball. As I've pointed out, the feminine nature of the places where the heroes achieve self-fulfillment supports the Freudian view of those heroes. This is particularly evident when the young hero supplants the old, to the acclamation of the fans in the maternal seats. When Pete Rose passed Ty Cobb, when Hank Aaron passed Ruth, the "great container" approved emphatically of the son who had just deposed the father, and it's no accident that everybody wanted those depositions to happen in each young hero's home park—as, fortunately for us and our myth, they did.

C. The Figures

The archetypal figures of baseball are the traditional ones, divided equally between Dionysiacs and Apollonians. The productive Dionysiac (Babe Ruth) uses his energy and strength to successfully achieve his goal; the destructive or misdirected Dionysiac (Hack Wilson) may be just as strong, but he is, literally, a loose cannon. The failure (Vic Wertz in 1954) has the proper goal, but insufficient strength. The orderly and intelligent Apollonian may be productive in two roles, that of sage (Tony LaRussa) or trickster (Casey Stengel); his negative incarnation is the type having little order or intelligence, the fool.

Of course, a player may wear more than one of these hats in a mythic life, or even at the same moment: as I've said, the fast ball pitcher who ages and must learn strategy has moved from productive Dionysiac to crafty Apollonian, and there are probably many examples of the productive Dionysiac (several in the Reds' bullpen) who is also an Apollonian fool. You can be a sage on the Apollonian side and a destructive Dionysiac, too; look at John McGraw. Fillers of the three negative "slots" (destructive Dionysiac, Dionysiac failure, and Apollonian fool) are always players who have lapsed, for a season or even for a split-second: this is because Utopia is impatient with heroes who don't maintain the high standard that got them there in the first place. Once again, these six archetypes may be complicated in six more ways, as follows:

Mask-Wearers. An individual who belongs in one archetype may pretend he is in another. When Eddie Collins pretended to have a limp and stole second on the next pitch, he was wearing the mask of a failed Dionysiac when in fact he was a productive one. Whenever Casey (the grizzled one, not the mighty) played the fool—even under oath and before Congress—he always knew exactly what he was doing, and his record as a manager indicates he was really a sage. Dizzy Dean liked to thank God for his strong arm and his weak mind; he wasn't serious. Collins, Stengel, and Dean, of course, were tricksters; most mask-wearers are.

Role-Changers. The hero who moves from one archetype to another during his mythic life is a role-changer, like the aforementioned pitcher who loses his fastball and has to learn pitchers' poker. Hack Wilson was one of the most productive Dionysiacs in history shortly before he became one of the most destructive and misdirected. Steve Howe went from productive Dionysiac to misdirected and back to productive again, and the final word may not be in on him yet, or on Pascual Perez, presently languishing in the Underworld.

Youth and Age. We view exceptionally young or old players differently, in a sense creating a variation on the archetype they represent. If they produce, we like them better; if they fail, we feel sorrier for them. While we are sympathetic to the very young and the very old regardless of whether they're Dionysiacs or Apollonians, there is a tendency to have more sympathy for the young Apollonian (he's supposed to be strong, but he's not supposed to be wise) and for the old Dionysiac (we expect him to be smarter by now, but also weaker). The Apollonian kid who's unusually mature, like Doc Gooden in his rookie year, will win us over as surely as the fading Dionysiac: Johnny Mize, Nolan Ryan. Nonetheless, we remain a generous lot, and we also give a little bit of extra credit to the young Dionysiac (Ott) and the old Apollonian (Seaver).

Martyrs and Pariahs. When a hero is forced out of the game in mid-myth even though he should be still entirely capable of playing it on the Utopian level, he is either a martyr or a pariah. The martyr is always at least badly injured (Herb Score, Tony Conigliaro, Dave Dravecky) or killed outright (Roberto Clemente, Lou Gehrig). The pariah, a sinner against some part of the Utopian code, is banished to the Underworld and told to forget all about Valhalla (Joe Jackson, Pete Rose). However, here it's important to recognize that archetypes are always imposed upon individuals according to the imposer's location. In other words, the particular ethics of the athlete's time, place and cultural group will determine whether or not a hero should or should not be reclassified a pariah, and there are many who remain convinced that both Jackson and Rose should be thought of as martyrs instead. For these dissenters, Rose and Jackson already are in Valhalla, and what any rubber-stamping Cooperstown should choose to do in future is beside the point.

D. The Tools

There are not many physical tools in baseball, and one, the ball, is always being replaced, but the other two major tools (aside from the ones of ignorance), the bat and the glove, are often of great importance to the hero. Every hitter normally has a favorite bat, or "lance," and pitchers and fielders usually break in and keep a single glove, or "cup." In part, this is a practical matter, simply the player's desire to use the tool with which he's most comfortable, but in part it's magic, and in fact it's as magic that one particular ball may become vital to the hero. Whenever a hitter gets his thousandth hit (or his first), the game is officially stopped so that he may given that particular ball, and the no-hit pitcher always keeps the last ball he threw in the game. Souvenir or talisman? You make the call.

Other "tools" of the mythical trade are the palladium, a good luck charm which will protect the fortunes of an entire group (the San Diego chicken), the amulet, which brings luck to the individual who has it (Lefty Gomez' button collection), and the incantation, which can either help the chanter or hinder his opponent.

For some reason, chants designed to help are usually chanted by groups ("Let's Go Mets!", so very successful in 1993), while devilish spells are more often intoned by a single mystic, although they may be directed at either an individual (possibly an umpire) or an entire team.

One example of the incantation designed to harm is the following, inflicted by Dizzy Dean on the very, very superstitious Hughie Critz:

> He invaded the dugout with this cat, a particularly black and sinister beast. He pointed its nose at Hughie Critz, an impressionable little fellow from Mississippi, and started making all kinds of hex signs and mumbo passes in Hughie's direction.
>
> "Cat, get Critz," said Mr. Dean. "Critz, get jinxed. Zmmmmm."

Mr. Critz looked around for the nearest exit and vanished into the clubhouse.

Mr. Dean seemed satisfied. "That got him," he said.

(*New York Times*, 17 July 1934: 32)

The uses of amulets are too numerous to rehearse, as are the various rituals designed to bring success—Wade Boggs' chicken diet, Tug McGraw slapping his thigh with his glove, the same Hughie Critz' habit of picking up pebbles in the infield with a mysterious and driven purpose that nearly drove his manager, John McGraw, crazy. McGraw himself felt that there was a negative palladium, a curse that could destroy the whole team's chances, in the appearance of a horseshoe of flowers, and he never let one into the Polo Grounds no matter how emotional the ceremony.

On the other hand, the Chicago Cubs made a tragic mistake in 1945: they refused to allow a *good* palladium, barowner Billy Sianis' goat, into their less-than-friendly confines for the world series. Sianis and the goat cursed them, and, of course, they haven't won since. In 1984, Dallas Green, who was then the Cubs' GM, tried to square things: he asked Sianis' nephew to bring in a descendant of the goat (Sianis had died, and so had the original goat) on opening day. The nephew did, a fuss was made, and the Cubs won the NL East. They went no further, however; too little, it seems, too late.

E. Localized Archetypes

When the archetypal figures become localized (embodied in a place, time or culture), there is the potential for conflict. A productive Dionysiac is only that, a static figure, until he faces another such in combat: then he becomes a hero to his worshippers, a rival/villain to the other guy's. These contests can be defined by time (was Ted Williams a better hitter than Babe Ruth?), by place (was Williams a more valuable player than Joe DiMaggio?), or by cultural group (was either Hank Aaron or Sadahurah Oh better than any one of the above three?). In a real sense, neither drama nor ethics enters into the myth-making process until you have two combatants or two teams, each manifesting the same universal archetypes.

In any contest, and particularly when it is between old rivals, every fan will agree on the archetypes the players fill, but there will be no agreement on which is "good," which "bad." As soon as our heroes are given different locations, they are given new archetypes, agonistic ones, and now the game begins.

Now I would like to examine some of baseball's manifested archetypes in greater detail.

Chapter 8

DIONYSUS AND APOLLO:
THE TWO GREAT GODS,
BABE RUTH AND WALTER JOHNSON

The two complementary sides or "shadows" that make up both the great mother and the omnipotent father are variously labeled. The most common terms for this dichotomy in the Orient are yin and yang. Jung uses anima and animus, and Nietzsche, as I've said, coins the terms Apollonian and Dionysiac. While I'm certainly not trying to suggest that these paired terms are precisely synonymous, they do all describe, with different emphases, the difference between the great feminine and masculine archetypes, and, for my purpose, Nietzsche's distinction is the most useful.

I'd like to begin my discussion of baseball's archetypal figures with two men who may very well represent these polar extremes better than any other ballplayers in the game's history: Ruth was baseball's ultimate Dionysiac, Johnson its perfect Apollonian. In Nietzsche the Apollonian impulse, like the god for which it is named, is orderly, balanced, and moderate, filled with the illuminating light of civilized reason:

> As a moral deity Apollo demands self-control from his people and, in order to observe such self-control, a knowledge of self.... accompanied by the imperatives, "Know thyself," and "Nothing too much." (34)

The Dionysiac thrust is a good deal less temperate. Far from trying to control the self, the Dionysiac hero tries to lose it, to re-assimilate into the disorderly material of creation: the votary of Dionysus, preferring wild faith to rational structure, will dissolve himself in nature; he is, in the term's

79

original sense, "dissolute." The Apollonian, religiously following orderly "codes of conduct," is a sportsman and a role-model; the Dionysiac, just as religiously, parties.

Like any other real fan, Nietzsche seems more interested in Dionysiac heroes than in Apollonian ones; he writes more about the Dionysiac impulse than he does about the Apollonian, making much of the spontaneous and natural qualities of the former. It was common to deify Ruth—Harry Hooper said that he "saw a man transformed from a human being into something pretty close to a god" (Ritter 145)—and Rube Bressler, presumably unconsciously, made Ruth's pure Dionysiac energy sound like the Fisher King himself:

> There was only one Babe Ruth. He went on the ball field like he was playing in a cow pasture, with cows for an audience.... He played by instinct, sheer instinct. He wasn't smart, he didn't have any education, but he never made a wrong move on a baseball field.
> He was like a damn animal. He had that instinct. They know when it's going to rain, things like that. Nature, that was Ruth! (Ritter 206)

Still, the baseball Apollonian has also had his advocates, particularly in American culture around the early part of the century, and Johnson was nearly eight years older than Ruth; and this is a good time to note that the Western view of the Apollonian-Dionysiac opposition (and particularly the American version of that Western view) has been complicated, if not compromised, by ethics.

Taken in and of themselves, Dionysiacs and Apollonians are not morally defined; they are just archetypes, figures which contain conflicting human qualities. There is no reason to say that one is good, the other bad, and in fact, that doesn't make sense; William Blake took pains to point out that his Tyger was neither worse nor better than his Lamb, and one of his better-known lines is, "without contraries, there is no progression." Still, in the West, the savage, physical figure (Caliban in Shakespeare's *The Tempest*) is usually viewed as wrong, the spiritual one (Ariel in the same play) as right. Dionysiacs are strong, physical, instinctual, and unthinking; we normally prefer orderly and rational Apollonians just as we elevate reason above instinct, or soul over body. The ultimate Apollonian in conventional Western myth is the knight in shining armor, the sagacious and spiritual hero who preserves the very chaste fair lady from the ultimate Dionysiac, the dragon.

The attachment of an ethical sub-text to the legitimate archetypal opposition of Dionysiac and Apollonian makes little sense, but that's irrelevant; this is the Western tradition, and we seem to be stuck with it. Therefore, when we look back on the heroic images of Ruth and Johnson, we will always feel a little embarrassed by the former, a little inclined to think of the latter as "better." This is true of our view of other Apollonians, too, and other Dionysiacs.

For a good sketch of the Apollonian ideal in America, a culture in which this moral bias is more pronounced than it is in many other Western places, you can turn to the Frank Merriwell stories, or to the language of that old muscular Christian, Teddy Roosevelt, as it's inscribed in the lobby of his Museum of Natural History in New York City, under the title YOUTH:

> I WANT TO SEE YOU GAME BOYS I WANT TO SEE YOU BRAVE AND MANLY AND I ALSO WANT TO SEE YOU GENTLE AND TENDER.
> BE PRACTICAL AS WELL AS GENEROUS IN YOUR IDEALS KEEP YOUR EYES ON THE STARS AND KEEP YOUR FEET ON THE GROUND.
> COURAGE HARD WORK SELF MASTERY AND INTELLIGENT EFFORT ARE ALL ESSENTIAL TO A SUCCESSFUL LIFE.
> CHARACTER IN THE LONG RUN IS THE DECISIVE FACTOR IN THE LIFE OF INDIVIDUAL AND OF NATION ALIKE.

This is a good abstract of the Apollonian code (which apparently did not involve careful punctuation), and it's not hard to see that Walter Johnson, who was a rookie and a sophomore pitching in Washington during Roosevelt's administration, fills this bill.

If the Babe was supposed to be all instinct, an elemental natural force, then Johnson was, or was thought to be, a near-saint, a chivalric figure, an Arthurian knight like Perceval. The sentimental comments made about him by those who knew him could have kept Hallmark Cards in business for years. Sometimes it seemed as though you were required to mine the Boy Scout Oath for at least one adjective before you were allowed to describe Walter Johnson. Sam Crawford said he was "a wonderful man in every way. Warm, and friendly, and wouldn't hurt a soul" (Ritter 57). Bill James, comparing him to Stan Musial, Matty and Lou Gehrig, said Johnson was "a gentleman...worthy of admiration" (372). He reminds you of a later Apollonian, Ernest Hemingway's DiMaggio from *The Old Man and the Sea*, who does everything well but, more importantly, "does all things perfectly."

Walter was from the proper side of the Olympian tracks; Mr. Johnson's was the more sedate neighborhood, the quiet block where the housepaint never peeled and the residents mowed their lawns every Saturday. Ruth, on the other hand, lived in the noisy end of town, and if somebody dropped a couple of empty beer cans in his driveway he didn't much care.

Different heroic types though they were, they were both lionized, and, I would contend, by everybody. In other words, the vast difference between their heroic images never resulted in one being much preferred to the other—they simply represented different aspects of each of us, id and superego if you like, or, again, anima and animus, and we were willing to accept them both. It's unsurprising that they were both included in the initial group of five installed in our official Cooperstown Valhalla. But what may be most interesting about the two men is the public response to the last great achievements of their mythic lives, when citizen Ruth was 40 and Johnson the mere man was 36.

Although he pitched for three more years and even won two more post-season games, Johnson's last truly memorable triumph came in winning the final game of the 1924 Series in four innings of relief. Ruth was well past his prime when he was playing for the Braves in early 1935, but a week before he walked off the field for good he hit three home runs in one game, the last two off Guy Bush, the pitcher who had been razzing him from the bench in Wrigley in the 1932 Series. His third home run was the longest ever hit at Forbes Field. It cleared the stands on the fly, bounced on the roof of one house, hit another, and ended in an empty lot, 600 feet away, making it even longer than the legendary homer in Tampa in 1919. Guy Bush said later he would never be able to forget it, and permitted himself a familiar cliche. "It's probably still going," he said (Creamer 397).

As this synopsis suggests, Johnson's triumph was Apollonian—he came in to relieve a team, to douse a threatening fire, to keep an orderly structure from collapsing. Ruth's was as powerfully and unstrategically Dionysiac as you can get, and the fact that this aging hero was reborn in the month of May was not mythically inappropriate.

After Johnson won that seventh game the city of Washington went nuts, indulging in what might have been the most enthusiastic celebration of a Series win in history. It started, of course, at the park, where the fans stampeded the players, and the Times reported that Earl McNeely "was thumped and pummeled and hugged and reached the bench a very crushed young man." Downtown, thousands of people soon filled the streets, blowing horns, shaking rattles, throwing confetti and crumpled paper out of windows, and even firing pistols, making a racket that outdid any New Year's Eve. Local theaters were forced to cancel performances because nobody could hear the actors' lines. An impromptu motorcade, klaxons blaring, was formed on Pennsylvania Avenue; soon there were at least a thousand cars, and the trolleys were forced to stop running. By morning, the confetti and paper thrown from offices was several inches deep in the streets.

The writers whooped in print. Will Wedge, who covered the Giants for the *New York Sun*, said that, even considering the high quality of play in the Series, "the baseball part of it goes by the board in face of the obvious sentimental drama. It was as if staged by Belasco and even more realistic.... It was the World Series with the storybook ending. Righteousness prevailed. Walter Johnson, spotless character...at last came into the spotlight" (11 Oct. 1924).

If we move over to the National League in the spring of 1935, we'll find that, in the games just before his great curtain call, much as an early tremor will warn a seismologist about an earthquake, old Dionysus had given everybody hints of what he was about to do. For two days in a row Ruth had hit balls that, but for Paul Waner's fielding, would have been extra-base hits even with an old man running. Now on Saturday he hit three out of the park, the last one, Ruth's last home run in any game anywhere, going farther than any of the many hundreds he'd hit before. The papers should have gone crazy.

But they *didn't*. The *New York Times* printed a box on page one of next day's Sunday edition giving sports results, but this was their standard procedure, and here's what they reported, in their editorial order of importance: Lawson Little won the British Open, and Henry Picard won the Metropolitan at Great Neck; with F.D.R. watching from the stands, Penn outrowed Navy and Harvard at a regatta at Annapolis; Rosemont won the Withers at Belmont; the Yankees took two from the Browns, the Giants beat the Cubs, the Dodgers lost, and "Babe Ruth hit three home runs, but the Braves were defeated by the Pirates, 11 to 7." In that order. Complete details in Section #5.

The story in Section #5 was not the lead, not close. It appeared at the very bottom of the first page of that section, and it was hardly more than 200 words long. At least it indicated that the fans in Pittsburgh had some idea of what they were witnessing:

> Rising to the glorious heights of his heyday, Babe Ruth, the sultan of swat, crashed out three home runs against the Pittsburgh Pirates today.
>
> The stands rocked with cheers for the mighty Babe as he enjoyed a field day at the expense of pitchers Red Lucas and Guy Bush, getting a single besides the three circuit blows in four times at bat and driving in altogether six runs.
>
> Ruth left the game amid an ovation at the end of the Braves' half of the seventh inning and after his third

home run—a prodigious clout that carried clear over the right-field grandstand, bounded into the street and rolled into Schenley Park. Baseball men said it was the longest drive ever made at Forbes Field. (26 May 1935)

Ruth had indeed "risen" again, and although he'd done so for the last time, he had done so more thoroughly and dramatically than any baseball hero ever has, before, since, and probably in the future.

It's inexplicable. Why did none of the writers find anything characteristic, or important, or moving in Ruth's incredible swan song? At 40, Ruth was literally on his last legs. In early May, running hard for a long fly, his heart had pounded so furiously he'd worried seriously that he might drop. Afterwards he told friends about it and said he knew he'd better quit soon. The huge discrepancy between the Babe's obvious physical deterioration and his heroic three-homer outburst should have made the baseball public react like the Parisians who met Lindbergh at Le Bourget.

Johnson's story was similar. Even though he was the game's dominant pitcher in 1924, and despite the fact that he'd win twenty again in 1925 and pitch for two more years after that, he was only one month shy of his 37th birthday when he walked to the mound that afternoon in 1924, and everybody thought it was his last chance to win a Series game. For the public, then, for us, the situations were virtually identical—in each case, one of the five greatest players in the history of the sport up to then had performed heroically one last time. Why was so much made of Johnson's heroism, so little of Ruth's?

I believe it has to do with the differences between Ruth and Johnson as heroes—the differences between the Apollonian and the Dionysiac. The Dionysiac hero is a divinity of nature and in nature, a figure symbolized by the annually resurrected Fisher King (note that the Pittsburgh reporter said Ruth had "risen again"); like the Fisher King, the Dionysiac hero can't die. Ruth is "omnipotent," Ruth is "god," Ruth is "nature"—he is not vulnerable, not someone we need worry about. He is someone of whom we expect superhuman achievement, regularly and always. Most important, like a god on Olympus or a hero on the Greek stage, he is someone with whom we cannot conveniently identify. We may adore him, but we can never really imagine being quite his size. "The Ruth is mighty," Heywood Broun said, intentionally using the diction of the Old Testament, "and shall prevail." Jahweh may be worshiped, but it is both hubristic and impossible to emulate Him.

The Apollonian hero, on the other hand, is an orderly individual. He has the perfectly human dimensions of Leonardo's drawing of man. His model is neither the unapproachable God of the whirlwind nor the naturally regenerative Fisher King, but the Christ. The Apollonian adheres to codes which are humanly realizable; in other words, you can identify with the Apollonian hero.

The fact that the Apollonian figure is more human than the Dionysiac also means there is in him more potential for failure; we don't always assume he will make it. Ruth's great day in 1935 was ignored because that was Ruth, and, even at 40, what else did you expect? Johnson's four-inning stint in 1924 was taken to heart for two reasons: one, we could all see ourselves walking out from that bullpen to that mound; two, Johnson might have failed, as he already had in games one and five. The Dionysiac hero is almost a god, the God of the Old Testament; the Apollonian is more a saintly man, one who resembles the Christ of the more recent portion of the same book.

Chapter 9

APOLLO AND DIONYSUS: DIVISIONS

While Ruth is a pure example of the powerfully productive Dionysiac, Johnson a perfect manifestation of the balanced and orderly productive Apollonian, there are other archetypes which must be subsumed under these two large headings. If his enormous energy is misdirected, the Dionysiac becomes destructive, harming his (and his team's) goals.

Please remember that I'm not talking about the life of the individual, rather the life of the mythic figure: Ed Delahanty and Len Koenecke both hit .300 the year before their personal recklessness killed them, and an editorial memorializing Billy Martin in the *New York Times* said that while "inside a baseball stadium he came as close as he ever did to...self-control," outside there was "another world...in which his pugnacity...produced behavior as pathetic as it was predictable" (27 Dec. 1989: A24). In fact, "pugnacity" is as good a term as any for the destructive Dionysiac, and Martin himself provides a fascinating illustration here. In the renowned pine-tar incident, Martin, often misdirected on the field, was downright Apollonian in his cleverness, but the ordinarily composed Apollonian, George Brett, was transformed into pure destructive energy. On that occasion, Martin called up the beast in Brett as surely as if he'd been Iago working on Othello.

The archetypal uniform Martin most often wore on the field was that of the crafty trickster, an Apollonian guise (and often disguise). The trickster, despite the connotations of his name and the fact that many mythical tricksters are bad guys, is a productive force; if the pure Apollonian wins ball games with sportsmanlike skill and errorless play, the trickster wins them with craft. It should be added that, almost all the time, this craft breaks no rules (again, look at the pine-tar incident); that's because, in baseball, a man in blue is almost always in position to see exactly what the trickster is doing. What the baseball trickster does is to encourage blunders, to make them much more possible: the catcher who positions himself or his glove so that the ump will mistakenly call a ball a strike, the outfielder who pretends to see a ball he's lost to hold the runner. All managers, by the way, from Mack to LaRussa, are tricksters.

Although his dangerously aggressive style obviously made him Dionysiac, Ty Cobb was essentially a trickster, as Tristram Coffin (and Cobb himself) recognized: when asked for his credo, Cobb just said, "scheme, scheme, and keep on scheming" (Stump 175). Leverett Smith agreed with Cobb's assessment when he said, "Cobb was a brainy player, Ruth a brawny one," recognizing that tricksters *are* Apollonians (75). Cobb's fury was certainly Dionysiac, but even that fury was subordinated to mind when Cobb played.

Craft is not necessarily (or even logically) yoked to aggression, and tricksters can be appealing, even downright lovable. If you took the traditional Apollonian "nice guy" and added a little fruitful mischief, you might get Herman "Germany" Schaefer.

Herman was a man of many nicknames, starting out his career as "Middles," and then "Noodles," before being given the one that stuck, "Germany"—although, after the start of World War I, he dropped "Germany," first for "Prince" (possibly because he was, along with his cohort Nick Altrock, one of the first players to be called a "clown prince"), then for "Liberty." Although today he is remembered chiefly as an eccentric, he was a lot smarter than people thought.

Some of Schaefer's jokes were just that, the pranks of a compulsive laugh-seeker, like the time he caught an ump asleep at a table in the back room of a Chicago bar. The Detroit writer Malcolm W. Bingay was Schaefer's main chronicler, and he tells the story in the voice of his Lardneresque character, Iffy the Dopester. The back room in question, a summer kitchen, had been added to the building, and a drainpipe which used to be outside remained on what now was an interior wall:

Now into the place one night came old Jack Sheridan, famed in song and story as an umpire. In the winter months when the season was over, Jack worked in Chicago as an undertaker. He called 'em in the summer and he buried 'em in the winter. And he did something else. As soon as the baseball schedule had run its course, Jack would settle right down to catch up on his fall drinking.

Well, this night Schaef found Jack back in that summer kitchen sound asleep, sitting on a hard-bottomed kitchen chair. His ear was nestled against the rough and rusty edge of the old drainpipe, just as comfy as though it were a silken cushion. That was enough for Schaef. He climbed up through the hole in the ceiling to the old roof and found the other end of the drainpipe.

Pouring into his ear Jack heard a terrible voice. "Jack Sheridan," it roared, "your time has came!"

Jack Sheridan got right up out of that chair and made the distance to the bar in nothing flat. He downed a couple and stood there waiting to determine, in his own mind, whether it was just something he had et.

After a while he went back to the summer-kitchen seat—and fell sound asleep once more, with his ear again resting on the drainpipe. For the second time Schaefer climbed the ladder and for the second time there came into Jack's ear the voice from the tomb: "Jack Sheridan, your time has came!"

Jack went right out onto Clark Street in such a hurry he went through Joe Cantillon's Japanese screen, which Joe prized very much as a work of art. (176)

More often, though, Schaefer's gags had a legitimate purpose. A notoriously weak power-hitter, he came to the plate once against Rube Waddell. Schaeffer was a genuine Apollonian, a clever man; the hard-throwing Waddell was a Dionysiac who was so dim some thought him handicapped. An ideal situation for a psych job, possibly like the one the trickster Cobb used on his friend, the illiterate Joe Jackson, when he pretended to be angry with him in the last months of the 1911 season (Cobb, who later admitted the anger was both feigned and calculated, wanted the batting title; he got it). At any rate, Schaefer consecutively took two of Waddell's hard strikes, then calmly told the Rube he was going to hit the next one out. No one knows if Waddell got rattled, but Schaefer *did* hit a home run on the next pitch, and there's little doubt that he knew his bravado *might* have rattled the great hayseed. Schaefer, in fact, had done exactly the same thing in the previous season, calling and then hitting one off Doc White of the White Sox. It seems to have been a favorite ploy, akin to the one used by trickster Stengel when he sent an old and fat Johnny Mize lumbering toward second on a steal and didn't even draw a throw.

Schaefer's greatest moment as a trickster, though, was the time he himself stole second—and then first, and then second again. Davy Jones told the story to Larry Ritter:

> We were playing Cleveland and the score was tied in a late inning. I was on third base, Schaefer on first, and Crawford was at bat. Before the pitcher wound up, Schaefer flashed me the sign for the double steal.... Well, the pitcher wound up and pitched, and sure enough Schaefer stole second. But I had to stay right where I was, on third, because...the Cleveland catcher.... refused to throw to second, knowing I'd probably make it home if he did.
>
> So now we had men on second and third. Well, on the next pitch Schaefer yelled, "Let's try it again!" And with a blood-curdling shout he took off like a wild Indian *back to first base,* and dove in headfirst in a cloud of dust. He figured the catcher might throw to first—since he evidently wouldn't throw to second—and then I could come home same as before.
>
> But nothing happened. Nothing at all... Everybody just stood there and watched Schaefer, with their mouths open, not knowing what the devil was going on. Me, too. Even if the catcher had thrown to first, I was too stunned to move, I'll tell you that....
>
> So there we were, back where we started, with Schaefer on first and me on third. And on the next pitch darned if he didn't let out another war whoop and take off *again* for second base. By this time the Cleveland catcher

evidently had enough, because he finally threw to second to get Schaefer, and when he did I took off for home and both of us were safe.

It's obvious that when he stole first Schaefer was after runs, not laughs, and it's also obvious that his strategy worked. It should be added that the umpires checked the rule book before allowing the play to stand, and that nothing was found forbidding running the bases backwards. Schaefer undoubtedly knew this. The rules were changed shortly afterward, as a direct result of this play.

Schaefer was an aggressive ballplayer (he and Cal Griffith were once suspended for protesting a bad call) who knew the game. He was a good coach who once even wrote an article on coaching. Had he not died young, this player/coach who had John McGraw's respect might well have ended up managing a major league club. Still, his obit in the *New York Times* on May 17, 1919, has this sub-head: "Baseball Comedian Passes Away." Once you've been assigned an archetypal "slot," it's very difficult to get the public to view you in any other way.

The two last archetypal divisions or categories, one Dionysiac and one Apollonian, are the negatives or "shadows" of the primary ones. The "shadow" of the productive Dionysiac is the unproductive one, the failure; the "shadow" of the sagacious Apollonian is the fool. Of course, failure and folly are necessarily very temporary among professional ballplayers, who would be unable to keep their jobs if they fell permanently into these archetypal categories: this means that most of these "losers" are losers only for a day. When I speak of failure, then, I'm speaking of the athlete whose best physical effort at a particular moment isn't quite good enough; by fool, the one whose mental lapse proves costly. Ralph Branca tried as hard as he could to throw the ball past Bob Thomson, and, fictionally speaking, neither Roy Hobbs nor the mighty Casey wanted to fan; the runner who leaves his base for the dugout because he mistakenly thinks the side has been retired will probably do that only once. Still, such lapses are memorable enough to deserve archetypal categories. As George Grella says, in baseball,

> The flaws, the failures, the defeats...live the longest.
> Merkle's boner, Snodgrass's muff, Mickey Owens' dropped
> third strike will endure forever in the memory of the fans
> and the unforgiving history of the game; the good such
> men have done is interred with their bones. (273)

Of the three figures Grella names, two (Owen and
Snodgrass) are failures, while the other (Merkle) is a fool. In
the bottom of the ninth, Owen dropped a difficult pitch
(Hugh Casey had thrown either a knuckler or an out-and-out
spitter) and Tommy Henrich, who should have struck out and
ended the game, went to first: but nobody scored on the play,
the Dodgers still had two outs, there was only one man on
(and he was on first), and the Dodgers had a one-run lead.
Give Owen a break; it was *Casey* who allowed the four
subsequent runs. Nonetheless, Owen enters baseball myth as
the goat, the physical failure. Snodgrass was certainly more
culpable, since he dropped a very high, very lazy, very easy
fly ball. Still, although the error put on a man on *second*
(and with nobody out), the situation was similar: it was the
final inning (the tenth, in this case) and the Giants were up
by one. The Red Sox would still have to go some to win, and
they'd have to beat Christy Mathewson to do it. They did, of
course, on a single, a walk, and a long sacrifice (I'm leaving
out the other walk, strategic and intentional), this despite an
incredible catch that stole a triple from Harry Hooper—this
catch by Snodgrass. So—should Owen be accused of the
physical lapse that cost Brooklyn that game, and should
Snodgrass bear the blame for New York's loss in the 1912
series? Is there a conspiracy of pitchers here?

The same argument can probably be made in the sad
case of Fred Merkle, the young man who gave "bonehead" to
our vocabulary. In 1908, when he was mythically christened
with that name, Fred was only 19. It was his second year
with McGraw's rough-and-tumble club, but he had been used
very little; it's hard not to think of him on the bench in the
Polo Grounds for those two years, surviving as best he could,
a terrified kid. By contrast, in 1908 the Giants' first base
coach was Hall-of-Fame pitcher Joe McGinnity, then a big
37-year-old who was playing his last year under McGraw.

McGinnity was not only big, he was tough. His nickname was "Iron Man," and that was a nickname he'd earned.

Merkle's date with infamy came on on September 23, in a game at the Polo Grounds with the Cubs. Please note, before we go any further, that this game was played a full two weeks before the regular season ended. It was tied in the bottom of the ninth when Merkle singled Harry McCormick to third. Far from encouraging the 19-year-old who had come close to batting in the winning run, McGinnity, standing right next to him, started to berate him; whether there was bad blood, nobody knows, but in any case, McGinnity called Merkle a stupid rookie and warned him to do exactly what he was told to do.

The next man up was Al Bridwell, who singled McCormick home, and McGinnity got excited. He started yelling, "Home, Harry, home!," yelling at the runner racing in from third, who had been with the club only half a season, but who had played as a regular during that time and who had been, comparatively, around; in other words, McGinnity would have felt more comfortable with "Moose" McCormick (he was nearly 30) than he did with Merkle, the kid. Also, since McCormick had been around the league, he would have known that his real name was Harry. Merkle only knew him as Moose, and probably had no idea in hell what his coach was telling him to do when he said "go Home"—because Merkle, who had just been told to listen up, probably thought that command was for him.

Anyway, it's well known that Merkle ran directly "home" to the clubhouse, failing to touch second base, that Frank Chance called for a ball so that he could stand with it on second and insist that the game be forfeited, and that it was. Equally well known that when the game was replayed two weeks later it meant the pennant, and the Cubs won.

So who was at fault?

Certainly it seems unfair to cast all the stones at Merkle, who had a long career and even appears on the roster of Ruth's Yankees. It looks even more certain when you realize that a dozen games were played between September 23 that year and the end of the season. In a sense, if Merkle's Giants couldn't streak, it's too bad they didn't fold; one more loss during that stretch drive would have gotten poor "bonehead" (lifetime .273) off the hook.

The athlete who may be the biggest (in quotes) archetypal "fool" in baseball may deserve the label even less than Merkle deserves his of the flop. This man was a successful businessman, somebody who had decided not to go to Berkeley (he'd been accepted) because he liked to play; after he quit the game, however, he returned to his more cerebral interest, botany, and developed several new kinds of orchid. You might think he was the model for a villain in a James Bond movie. Instead, he was the guy who (they said) let fly balls bounce off his head and remained unperturbed when he ended up on third base with two of his offensive teammates.

The first part of that sketch of Babe Herman refers to his real life as an individual; the second, to the life of "Babe Herman," the cartoon character.

Herman was a smart man, as many mythical fools are (think of Yogi Berra), so he wasn't threatened by the fun the writers and fans were having, or, more properly, by the need they had to "fill" the fool's slot with him. He confessed he had once lost a fly in the sun, but said it had hit him in the shoulder. Why hadn't he set the record straight? "It made a better story," he said, "so I let it go."

In summary, if Babe Ruth and Walter Johnson are very good examples of the strong and productive Dionysiac and the productive and sagacious Apollonian, you can find individual "fillers" for the four other "slots" as follows: misdirected and destructive Dionysiacs, Billy Martin; failed Dionysiacs, Ralph Branca and the fictional Casey; crafty Apollonians, "Germany" Schaefer or Ty Cobb, and failed Apollonians, Fred Merkle and the best known and most maligned of all, Floyd "Babe" Herman.

Chapter 10

APOLLO AND DIONYSUS: VARIANTS

The Interrupted Journey: Martyrs and Pariahs

While there are plenty of ballplayers who never make it to Utopia and/or Valhalla because they haven't the skills, they are not relevant because, by definition, they're not heroes. When a genuine hero's journey is cut short it can happen in one of two ways: he can be martyred, or he can be drummed out of the game. The martyred hero, for whom the model is Adonis, inevitably goes to Valhalla; the disgraced one, or pariah, ends up in the Underworld. As always, these are locations for the mythic figure, not the real one. Pete Rose is in the Underworld and Dave Dravecky is in Valhalla, but both are alive as individuals.

The question of the pariah is a tough one, since the mythical villain is an agonistic archetype, the kind which usually appears only when one located myth confronts another. In other words, we may need to conclude that ethical distinctions never enter the archetypal figures *per se*, and that good and bad are relative, surfacing only when the pantheon splits and becomes plural, when the hero of the monomyth divides into the agonistic hero and rival. If that's the case, then, just as one team's villain is another one's hero, maybe one myth's pariah is another one's martyr; maybe the "code" of each game is localized.

The case of baseball's most famous pariah, far from answering this question, only asks it more clearly. Joe Jackson is officially a pariah, firmly residing in the Underworld and forever denied Valhalla, but there are large numbers of people who think him a martyr instead, and, for them, he's already in Valhalla. Bill James, for example, like Hughey Fullerton before him, hates Jackson's illiterate guts; Wilfrid Sheed (a much better writer than either of those two)

wants to see him in the Hall of Fame. It all boils down to
this: if there is such a thing as archetypal villainy, then
pariahs are possible, and Jackson may have to stay right
where he is; but if we *can't* find something like a categorical
imperative in myth, if morals turn out to be variable
according to geography, history, and culture, then maybe
Joe's case should be brought back into court. In any case,
and because of the ambivalence of the baseball myth on this
point, I've reserved consideration of pariahs for my discussion
of localized myth.

* * *

> The phone rung. It was his father, and he was dead.
> That was October 7.... He was not a bad fellow, no worse
> than most and probably better than some.
>
> —Mark Harris
> (*Bang the Drum Slowly* 242-43)

Adonics, or martyrs, present no such problem, since
devastating injury or early death is painfully final: if a fine
young pitcher loses his throwing arm to cancer, there is no
ambiguity about his status; he is through; he is mythically
dead. Fortunately, of course, there is the afterlife of Valhalla,
and he will be secure there. Once again, Valhalla need not be
the Hall of Fame itself; you can get there simply by being
permanently remembered as heroic. However, the most
obvious and well-known Adonics die outright. Sometimes the
death is sudden, like those of Clemente or Ray Chapman,
and sometimes it takes a couple of years, like that of Gehrig;
sometimes it even occurs after the athlete/hero's mythic life
is over, as in Christy Mathewson's case. However the hero is
stricken, though, after his death he is always made into not
just a hero, but a divinity. It's either remarkable or to be
expected that the eulogies of these men sound so similar that
if you had only the praise to go by you would be hard
pressed to identify the real individual beneath the Adonic
archetype. After Addie Joss died of meningitis two days after
his thirty-first birthday, Billy Sunday said this:

> He was one of the men who, by his gentlemanly manner, sterling manhood and unimpeachable honesty was an honor to the profession. He was one of those men who, by their character and manhood, have helped the game maintain its hold on the American people, from the President in the White House to the newsboys on the street, from the staid and dignified members of the Supreme Court to the huckster selling his wares from a wagon. (Jim Ingraham 29)

After Lou Gehrig went to the Mayo Clinic and was diagnosed as having a fatal disease, the *New York Times* said he'd left "a record of good sportsmanship and clean living that has been a shining example for every boy who ever stepped on a playing field" (22 June 1939: 27). After he died, New York Governor Lehman said "he...always stood for fair play and clean sport; he was a fine type of American whose example may well be followed by the youth of our state" (*Times*, 4 June 1941: 8). As David Voigt says, Gehrig was the "Galahad" of his era (214), and although it's obviously only coincidence, the Westchester County town he was buried in is Valhalla, New York.

Of all of baseball's martyrs, Roberto Clemente, who worked for urban kids and died on a charity mission, may have been biographically most worthy of the mythic divinity we've imposed upon him; Christy Mathewson, whose real life was much more at variance with his mythical one, may have been least worthy. Nevertheless, the language used to eulogize the two men appears cut from the same thesaurus. Speaking of Clemente, Governor Colon of Puerto Rico said "our youth have lost an idol," and his Secretary of State, directly referring to Clemente's immortality, said "we have with us today the spirit of a man who helped teach us how to become better citizens" (*New York Times*, 2 Jan. 1972: A5); after Matty died, the *New York Times* said he'd been "the idol of the nation's fandom over a span of more than two decades," and that he was "a symbol of the highest type of American sportsmanship" (8 Oct. 1925: 11).

All the notices for Matty's death were similar—Seymour quotes one that says "he played the game of life as he did the game of baseball, fighting hard, but always fair and honorable," and he mentions that Bucknell inducted him into its hall of fame (there was none in Cooperstown then) because he was "a conspicuous standard bearer of honesty and the best sportsmanship" (116). But Seymour also reminds us that the noble Matty once punched out a lemonade boy for making a crack about a fellow Giant, splitting the kid's lip (115). On that occasion, a complex and real individual had emerged from behind the fan-imposed mask, and the startled witnesses didn't much like it. One writer said that while Matty was "gentlemanly-appearing," what he'd done was "brutal," and the fans at the game (it was away, in Philly) nearly rioted. Still, as Seymour remarks, "this episode was not in keeping with the accepted stereotype of Mathewson and somehow got painted out during the process of portraying him as a paragon of virtue." He remained, as Seymour said, "an American folk hero unsurpassed in that era" (115), and he stays in Valhalla, whatever the facts of his real life, as a perfectly Apollonian Adonic: witness Greenberg's *The Celebrant*, the fine contemporary novel that actually compares Mathewson to Christ, or Harris' *Bang the Drum Slowly*, whose martyred player dies, as you've already noticed, on October 7, the date of Matty's own death.

Overachievers: Youth and Age

As I've said, the exceptionally young hero is presumed to be naive, not that far removed from the innocent Arcadia he's only recently left, and so we are particularly impressed if he seems wise, whereas the unusually old one must be, by the fact of his age, weaker than he was, and so we are more responsive to his feats of physical strength than we would have been had he been younger. The old athlete—"old" here means in his thirties—is sympathetic precisely *because* we see him as a figure in a myth, and because, in the context of that myth, he's dying. The best example of an old athlete astonishing us with his strength—resurrecting himself, really—remains Ruth's last home run, mentioned above, which may also have been his longest.

Kids with the sagacity of mature men are rarer, and, since their mythical lives lie all before them, less emotionally powerful for us. Mel Ott comes to mind, since that protege of John McGraw knew the game most thoroughly long before he was old enough to join the army or vote, probably before he was able to drive a car. The very young can also impress us with their strength—the slugging Ott, again—just as the athletically elderly may surprise us with their ability to think. The nickname they gave Stengel in his later years expresses our admiration for such heroes quite well: "The Old Professor," they called him.

Multiple Archetypal Personalities:
Role-Changers and Mask-Wearers

Once again, these are categories which invite moral scrutiny, even though there is nothing *inherently* ethical or unethical in changing your ways, even in pretense itself; the moral consideration usually enters in with regard to personal character or motive. Is your new role noble, an improvement, or does it follow a pitiable collapse like Hack Wilson's? Is the mask you wear designed to take unfair advantage of the people for whom you're wearing it, as Chick Gandil's was? At their most neutral, though, these archetypal shape-shifters aren't to be judged. If a pitcher becomes an outfielder or if a reliever becomes a starter, there is (or should be) neither praise nor stigma attached; and the honest mask-wearer is really just a trickster, working productively for his club.

Chapter 11

LOCALIZED BASEBALL ARCHETYPES

Place, Time, and Cultural Group

In everything that's gone before, you'll have noticed a peculiar dearth of discussion of baseball games themselves. This is because you can't have conflict (and therefore a contest) without location—without sending up your team from Shreveport, say, against the guys who have come over from Waco. Even though it's quite obvious that the universal pantheon of baseball heroes has to "split" into a number of similar groups in order to have games, and that the teams that play these games will come from different places, regional location is only one of three factors that must be considered in examining how we convert real people into manifestations of the archetypes; the other two factors are *temporal location* and *location in cultural group*.

To take the last first, it must be realized that baseball played in different cultures will be viewed differently by members of those cultures, and that this is a necessary given. Take four of baseball's main cultural "locations," Hispanic America, Black America, White America, and Japan, and then take the most famous sluggers from each, Roberto Clemente, Josh Gibson, Babe Ruth, and Sadaharu Oh. Starting with each culture's desire to view its own players as heroes, with their opposites as rivals or shadows, isn't it likely that a black American (whatever he may say) will think of Ruth as "the white Josh Gibson"? Additionally, as books on the subject have shown, the game is played according to different standards in both Latin America and Japan—in Japan, for example, a "hot dog" will be less tolerated than in the States, and god knows what they'd do to a child-injuring destructive Dionysiac like Vince Coleman. David Voigt makes a similar point about cultural divisions in this country when he says the early heroes for midwestern farmers were Honus Wagner and Walter Johnson, while "southern rednecks" preferred Joe Jackson. In contemporary American baseball, a conflict can be cultural as well as regional—L.A. vs. New York in the 1981 series, San Diego vs. Detroit in the 1984—but in general, cultural location is the least important of the three.

Location in time is important in two ways. First, there is what Roger Angell calls "the interior stadium," the place where images of old or even dead individuals remain mythically fresh and young, the place where Jim Brosnan's passionately dedicated "inner fan" can envision and measure Johnson and Gibson or Ty Cobb and Rickey Henderson as though they were all simultaneously in their prime. Second, there is the significance of temporal location when we look back on relatively distant history and try to determine whether the myth as handed down to us has any validity by our contemporary standards. Here again figures like those of Christy Mathewson and Joe Jackson are crucial; so is that of Cobb. The question we have to ask is really an ethical one. Are the morals by which these three have been judged still valid? Have we been fair?

To understand how their particular mythical archetypes were attached to these three individuals it will be necessary to take a look at their era. It was an era, as I've said, that still embraced muscular Christianity, which was itself a variety of American puritanism and contained, as the name suggests, both an Apollonian and a Dionysiac thrust. The problem was that, back then, sometimes the muscle got separated from the work of Christ and was applauded as a good in itself. Bill James, a Kansan, seems heir to this tradition; in any event, he perpetuates the belief in the virtue of a sportsman who is also a tough competitor in his *Historical Baseball Abstract*, in which he judges Mathewson, Cobb, and Jackson. James describes an old photo of Cobb with Matty:

> [Cobb] is holding what looks like an expensive overcoat, and he appears to be dragging it on the ground. His hat is jaunty and his smile is decidedly nervous, and he looks frankly a little bit crazy.

Cobb was then a five-time American League batting champion, with more or less seven seasons under his belt—and yet he was also a twenty-four-year-old hick from Nowhere, Georgia, a little in awe of Matty, of the photographers, of the crowd. He had no weapons, at that moment, to defend himself against his inadequacies—no spikes, no bat, no glove. He was so crude and unpolished that he must have felt that whenever they took those things away from him, he became nothing.... You can see it in his face, I think, that if he could just put on a uniform and go out on the field it would be such a relief to him, out where manners and taste and style were all defined by bases gained and bases lost. And everyone else, for a change, would have to apologize to him. (387-88)

This is a very revealing passage, entirely sympathetic to Cobb, a shy and innocent kid, only "a little bit crazy" but still reassuringly concerned with the important issues of gain and loss, a kid who shouldn't have to worry about "manners and taste and style"—and who will make those who do worry about those things apologize to him once he gets on the basepaths.

James' treatment of Jackson is just as interesting. He begins by admitting that Joe had only confessed to taking money, never to helping throw any games at all, but then he concludes his evaluation with a long, scathing and finally petty condemnation:

My own opinion as to whether or not Joe Jackson should be put in the Hall of Fame is that of course he should; it is only a question of priorities. I think there are some equally great players who should go in first.... Then, too, the players of the nineteenth century have never really gotten their due.... And then I think.... there should probably be better provisions made for people whose contributions to the game were not made on the field, like Grantland Rice, Barney Dreyfuss, Harry Pulliam.... And, too, we do not want to forget the many wonderful stars of the minor leagues.... When they are in we can turn our attention to such worthwhile players of our own memories

as Roger Maris.... And then, at last, when every honest
ballplayer who has ever played the game, at any level
from Babe Ruth ball through the majors, when every
coach, writer, umpire and organist who has helped to
make baseball the wonderful game that it is rather than
trying to destroy it with the poison of deceit, when each
has been given his due, then I think we should hold our
noses and make room for Joe Jackson to join the Hall of
Fame. (376)

Although James also says Jackson was "too stupid to
know exactly what was going on," now he concludes that his
diabolical plot was "to destroy" the "wonderful game" of
baseball "with the poison of deceit." As far as Bill James is
concerned, Jackson is the ultimate betrayer, and James
probably won't be satisfied until Dante's Satan grows a
fourth mouth so that Shoeless Joe can join Brutus, Cassius,
and Judas himself at the bottom of hell, being mumbled and
chewed throughout eternity. I don't think James is old
enough to have been the kid who supposedly asked Jackson
if it was so, but the shock of discovering Jackson's treachery
certainly seems to have convinced him he's not in Kansas
anymore.

Cobb, however, is different, and James is far from his
only apologist. Cobb *always* tried to win, and when a
champion is that aggressive, you can forgive him a little
psychopathic excess, the malicious slide that ends a catcher's
career, the savage killing of a man in an alleyway, or the
rather heavy-duty browbeating of his biographer, Al Stump.

There's something wrong with this ethical picture. Why
is Jackson vilified, Cobb lionized? The answer probably lies
in our admiration for the tenets of muscular Christianity in
our puritan past. When the Puritans made hard work a
virtue, it became concurrently virtuous for each man to
control his own economic destiny. This resulted in an
important separation between the pietist source of the work
ethic (the Christianity) and its pragmatic and secular side
(the muscle). As Max Weber says:

> The capitalist system so needs this devotion to the
> calling of making money, it is an attitude toward material
> goods so well suited to that system, so intimately bound
> up with the conditions of survival in the economic
> struggle for existence, that...it no longer needs the support
> of any religious forces. (72)

"Work ethic" was now accented on the first syllable;
Calvin had given place to Poor Richard. Still, the work ethic,
which had begun as an aspect of religion, remained a kind of
economic faith: the flavor of dogma was retained, and people
still blindly assumed that hard work was "the right thing to
do." Separated from conventional religious rules like the
Golden one, the work ethic could now embrace aggressive
and even ruthless behavior, and any survey of the great
industrialists of the late nineteenth century will show that it
did. The paradox here is that the work ethic was still an
article of quasi-faith, even though it now came more under
the heading of social Darwinism than of Calvinism or
Protestantism; the individual American father, no longer
running his own store, was in the home much less often, and
the kids were cared for by the mother. David Leverenz
suggests that this "vanished" or even "failed" father has
become a familiar obsession among those famous Americans
he calls our "psychic barometers," noting the cases of
Fitzgerald, Faulkner, and Hemingway (271, 259, 267). He
could easily have added Ty Cobb to this list, since Cobb's
father was killed by his mother in what may (or may not)
have been a tragic accident.

By the turn of the century, then, the work ethic no
longer had much to do with the Christian principles of
humility and charity, although everyone pretended, or
possibly believed, it was still a "good." Leverenz suggests
further that the young men of the times were Calvinists at
home, but that they became capitalists once they followed
their fathers to work:

> The...family in America repressed its aggressive
> sons...while the new mercantile culture encouraged those
> same sons in their aggressiveness. (268)

What has this moral inconsistency got to do with baseball? It provides an explanatory background for our tendency to judge athletes according to two different, and basically contradictory, codes, both of which are essentially Puritan. According to the older pietistic code, which is essentially that of orthodox religion, lying cannot be countenanced, neither can greed, and betrayal is probably the worst sin of all (again, see Dante). But according to the newer work ethic, which originated in the church but soon drifted its own distinctively different way, aggressive behavior is perfectly acceptable and even laudable as long as it achieves something for the aggressor. Jackson had the misfortune to be judged by the pietistic code. Cobb had the luck to be judged according to the work ethic.

Having said all this, it's undoubtedly flogging a very dead horse to cite all the writers who praise Cobb and damn Jackson. After all, Cobb did get more writers' votes than anybody else when he became the first member of the Hall of Fame, and Bill James is reasonably unequivocal in saying he'd like to see Jackson get in dead last. And if we ask two questions—"which great player was most aggressive," and "which great player was most crooked"—the survey is always going to say "Cobb" and "Jackson." Bill James is only one of the most recent Jackson-bashers; the tradition extends back to Hughey Fullerton, who scorned the illiterate hayseed even before the scandal broke, and who actually invented the disillusioned little kid who asked Joe to say it wasn't so, thus proving that the kid really couldn't have been James.

James' views, in any case, are mainstream; he is not a revisionist of myth; for him, a six-footer who loosens a kid's teeth and a player who tries to hurt anybody who stands in his way are not that bad, because they're true competitors, while someone who takes hush money but doesn't alter his performance is vile. In the climate of his time—terrible pay and frequent "fixing" of regular-season games—Joe Jackson may very well have thought that, although the choice was hard, he was doing the right thing. Maybe Donald Gropman is right. "In truth," he says, at the end of his book, "Joe Jackson's greatest crime was his innocence" (229).

Cultural differences do play a part in the creation of our heroes, and different historical eras do put the same individuals into different "slots," but neither of these phenomena of location has much to do with the creation of agonistic archetypes, molds for individuals who become, for us, either good or evil. Heroes and villains depend on *regional* location. Roger Clemens is a hero in Fenway, a villain at the Stadium. Sometimes the rivalry between two regions is heightened by the cultural differences between the two places, and then the heroes and villains seem more exaggerated than ever, but only once in the history of baseball has an intense regional rivalry been further heightened by close proximity.

From 1913 to 1957 a 20-minute subway ride would take you between working-class Brooklyn and the glitter of Manhattan, from raucous Ebbets Field to the comparatively sedate Polo Grounds or vice versa. The Red Sox-Yankee rivalry pales beside the old Dodger-Giant war. There was no particular cultural division between Bostonians and Manhattanites, for one thing, unless you want to say the former were more stuffy, the latter more continental; they were both upper-crust enough to be of interest not just to Bill James, but also to Henry.

Brooklyn and New York, however, were not social equals, and the additional factor—the most important factor in their unique rivalry, by far—was the fact that each team's park was so easily accessible to the other team's faithful. This meant that players couldn't count on the support of a home crowd during the years the two teams flourished in adjacent boroughs. Take the Dodger-Giant series that closed out the 1934 season at the Polo Grounds. That spring, Giant manager and first baseman Bill Terry made a crack the Brooklyn fans never forgave. The Giants had won everything the year before, taking the Series from Washington in six; the Dodgers, as usual, had floundered in the second division. When a reporter asked how much trouble he thought he'd get from Brooklyn, Terry joked, "Are they still in the league?"

Instant villain. Overnight, Terry was called the most hated man in Brooklyn, and the Dodger fans turned out in droves, both at Ebbets Field and across the river in the Polo Grounds. Their team had lost many more to the Giants than they had won that year, but when it came time to play that last two-game set, the Giants, in the thick of a tight pennant race, were exhausted. The stands were full for the first game, and about half the patrons were from exotic spots like Red Hook and Greenpoint; the Dodgers won. Now the Giants could only tie St. Louis to force a playoff. On the last day of the season, sensing revenge, the Brooklyn fans were back in even greater force, like sharks at a frenzy. The Dodgers won again. The villain Terry had been punished.

It goes without saying that Giant fans took a different view, thinking of Terry and his team as gallant heroes hounded and persecuted by an unruly mob. The Dodger-Giant rivalry was so heated that trades between the teams posed special problems. When Freddie Fitzsimmons went from New York to Brooklyn, he cried; Jackie Robinson, told the Dodgers had sent him to the Giants, just quit. And when the prototypical Dodger Leo Durocher replaced the ultimate Giant Mel Ott as manager, several New York fans loudly declared they'd never enter the Polo Grounds again.

Suffice it to say that the agonistic pattern was never clearer than when the Dodgers and the Giants were both in town; every Dodger hero was a villain in Harlem, every Giant star was non grata in Flatbush. And here a brief word should be said about the predicament of the members of the most victimized agonistic category, the judges.

Umpires

I noted that th'empire erred an' in gin'ral I must deplore an astonishin' lack in thrained scientific observation on th' part iv this officyal. He made a number iv grievous blundhers an' I was not surprised to larn fr'm a gintleman who set next to me that he (th' empire) had spint th' arly part iv his life as a fish in the Mammoth Cave iv Kentucky. I thried me best to show me disapproval iv his unscientific an' infamous methods be hittin' him over th' head with me umbrella as he left the grounds.

—Finley Peter Dunne ("Mr. Dooley")
("On Baseball" 252)

As Voigt points out, for the umps, "any decision made enemies" (227), since every decision had to go against somebody's batch of heroes. This was a particularly dangerous situation in Dodger-Giant games, since, when the emotions of a rivalry run this high, it becomes difficult to separate the real world from the mythical one. Take the events of July 12, 1938, in a little bar in Brooklyn, where a bunch of guys were hashing over that day's game at Ebbets Field. The bartender, Pat Diamond, was telling his pal, a postman named Robert Joyce, that the Dodgers stank. Joyce didn't like to hear that. He went home and loaded two revolvers, came back, and shot his friend. When an out-of-towner named Frank Krug tried to disarm him, he shot him, too. Diamond and Krug both died. When Ed Hughes wrote it up in the *Brooklyn Eagle*, he made the logical connection between this incident and the hazards of the umpirical profession:

> "Kill the ump!" has been the clarion call of the fan since the dawn of baseball. In any fair-thinking society, the umpire would be honored. But not in baseball. The arbiter's life has countless times been put in real jeopardy. (14 July 1938: 19)

While it's certainly true that the ump has often been in jeopardy, there's no available record of an actual murder, although there have been close calls. George Magerkurth was once attacked on the playing field by a fan who leapt from the bleachers, George Moriarty was once waylaid by a bunch of players under the stands, and one unfortunate ump had to leave a game to seek medical help after a fastballing fan with remarkable location threw a bottle that hit him in the groin. In an old issue of *Baseball Magazine*, F.E. Folsom offered an entertaining sketch of the life of the ump in the "good old days" before the First War. He presents his stories in annals fashion, and here is my summary of some of them:

> May 5, 1904—President Tebeau of Louisville was suspended for ten days by League President Grillo for

throwing Umpire Bauswine's clothing into the street and locking him out of his dressing room.

June 18, 1904—At Cincinnati, Umpire Moran was mobbed by bleacherites.

July 11, 1904—Outfielder John Thoney of Rochester assaulted Umpire Kelly on the field at Buffalo.

September 10, 1904—Manager Cantillon of Milwaukee assaulted Umpire Shuster at St. Paul.

November 23, 1904—Umpire Tom Brown was beaten and mobbed at Los Angeles.

June 10, 1905—Milwaukee forfeited their game to Indianapolis because the Milwaukee battery, Hickey and Wolf, plotted to hit the umpire with the ball.

June 16, 1905—Umpire Wood left the Springfield-South Bend game in the sixth inning because of incessant kicking by the players.

July 11, 1905—South Bend's manager and second baseman, Angus Grant, assaulted Umpire Rigler, and was promptly placed under arrest and taken to police headquarters in the patrol wagon.

July 13, 1905—Buffalo forfeited their game to Jersey City because, although Umpire Hassett was knocked down and beaten by Buffalo shortstop Nattress and other Buffalo players, Buffalo manager Stallings refused to put Nattress off the bench.

August 7, 1905—National League President Pulliam suspended Hans Wagner for three days and fined him $40 for throwing a ball at Umpire Bauswine.

August 17, 1905—At Toledo, Umpire Kane was pelted with eggs, mud, and cushions and escorted to his hotel by a police guard.

April 14, 1907—In the final game for the Cuban championship at Havana, Umpire Borrato gave his final decision with revolver in hand and then darted behind the line of police. The crowd charged, but the police and rural guards closed round and saved him.

July 13, 1907—A Western Association Umpire was assaulted during the eighth inning of the Webb City-Wichita game by players Painter, Milton, and Collins and so badly beaten that he was afterwards removed to a hospital. Policemen with drawn revolvers held the crowd from also attacking the umpire, whose name was Guthrie.

This sort of thing appears to have been going on from the Pacific highland to the New York island, and it illustrates the unique position of the judge in the agonistic archetype: he is always viewed as a villain by the side he sides against, but, oddly, never as a hero by the other side. The fans of the player or team in whose favor the decision has gone always imperiously assume that it is justice, simple and true; Solomonic judges are *expected* to be able to identify God's servants.

PART FOUR

LESSER

SPORTS

AND

CHRONICLERS

Chapter 12

LESSER SPORTS

It's common practice for the baseball faithful to decry the apostasy of those who prefer other sports. Wilfrid Sheed's tongue-in-cheek dismissal of all other games (through the title to which I refer above, *Baseball and Lesser Sports*) is one contemporary example; Thomas Boswell's list of the hundred reasons baseball is superior to football is another. While not everyone agrees with them (there are a few heretics out there), it can be argued that theirs is the strongest voice, that baseball remains our most national sporting myth. I'd like to eventually return to baseball with this notion in mind, but before I do it will be valuable to look at some of the "lesser" games played in this country. I see these other games as falling into three categories: games which, like baseball, are essentially American; games played, not by all Americans, but by particular cultural and economic groups; and finally universal games, those which are played world-wide. These categories need not be mutually exclusive, of course; boxing, a universal sport, has almost always been defined both by economic group (the poor) and by ethnic group (the disadvantaged—Irish, or Italian, or black, or Hispanic). On the other hand, yachting, always a rich man's sport, is also universal.

American Sports

Sociologists usually list the three most "American" sports in the same pecking order, as follows: baseball first, then football, finally basketball. They also usually define them in much the same way. To take two examples from the many available ones, Novak and Calhoun both speak of baseball first, saying it centers on individuality; then they turn to football, which Novak calls "violent" and "lawless"

(42) (Calhoun uses the word "intimidation" 184); then to basketball, which both say centers on "deception."

These distinctions, which have been repeated by so many other writers that they border on cliché, describe differences which say more about the differences of fans than about either the individual players or the heroes we make of them. The basketball fan, in other words, is likely to appreciate the trickster side of Michael Jordan (his "moves") more than his more conventional Dionysiac one (his strength) or his Apollonian one (his grace, his shooting skill); similarly, the football fan is traditionally most impressed by brute Dionysiac strength—"DE-fense! DE-fense!"

That these qualities—deception and macho power—are positive qualities to many Americans is shown by the popularity of football and basketball here. That we still lionize freedom and individuality above all other attributes, however, is at least suggested by the fact that Novak and Calhoun (again, among many others) *lead off* their discussions with baseball.

The degree of popularity of one of these lesser sports usually reflects the social climate. When the country was more hawkish than it is now, a couple of decades ago, observers felt that football had nudged aside baseball as the great American game; they undoubtedly would not say so now. Basketball will probably never move up from its third-place position unless the country begins to put a greater faith in wiliness as the most proper means of survival, to prefer the memory of Nixon to that of Ike.

In other words, there is probably a relatively greater premium placed on different archetypes in these three sports: in basketball, there are more tricksters; in football, more productive Dionysiacs, and in baseball, even discounting the glaring and godlike exception of the Great Ruth, more straightforward Apollonians. Even at this late stage in our history, it seems we prefer winning in nobility to success achieved through power or by deceit. Is this because Americans remain Puritan-prissy? "No woman of quality," says Thomas Boswell, "has ever preferred football to baseball" (*Washington Post*, 18 Jan. 1987: 29). Boswell's irony seems to label baseball as socially correct, maybe a little too proper to get muddy, but I think that's unfair both to his joke and to what Seymour's last book calls "the people's game": I think Boswell is simply saying that beauty really *does* prefer the normal individual to the steroidal beast, and I think he intends his "woman" to stand for the majority of American spectators, regardless of gender. To suggest that both basketball and football are essentially more *competitive* sports than baseball isn't as radical as it may sound; think of the enormously competitive Pete Rose in the 1975 Series, telling Carlton Fisk he was just glad to be there, happy to be part of the ceremony, and imagine the reaction of Tom Landry or Vince Lombardi were either managing him.

Remember that neither basketball nor football has a universal "hymn," an anthem that celebrates *the game itself* without localizing it in any way, and that, as I've said, conflict or agon is only possible after the mythical players have been given some sort of location. Baseball has its hymn, of course, and it's been remarked that it's sung by a woman who would much rather go out to the old ball game than be under a parasol, serenaded in a canoe on some river or lake. That woman, unquestionably one of quality, personifies all of us; she's the Kathleen ni Houlihan of this country as a whole.

Economically Located Sports

While I've previously spoken largely of localized groups as definable according to region, time, and culture, it is also possible to make economic distinctions, both between sports that occupy those three groups and between different sports themselves.

Whenever there is a measurable economic difference between different regions, the agon between the two regions will take this into account; I've mentioned the 1984 World Series between relatively rich San Diego and demonstrably poor Detroit, and part of the volatility of the response to that series must have come from the fact that the Detroit fans were very much aware of that difference. Economic factors play less a part when they are considered over time, but they exist in that context, too; think of the different image the

Dodgers have had since they moved from the bagels of Brooklyn to the salads and Napa Valley blush of L.A. Finally, economic distinctions appear in cultural groups, too; Arthur Ashe did not get to Wimbledon via the playing fields of Eton. As you can see, though, these economic factors are inevitably corollary, subsumed under other, more important ones; this is why I haven't dealt with them before.

When you turn to particular sports themselves, though, there is reason to introduce a new discussion, because some sports are available only to people with either much or some money. Yachting, of course, is a rich man's sport, and the ability of a brash *nouveau* like Ted Turner to break into it probably only underscores its unavailability to practically everybody on the planet; paraphrasing J.P. Morgan, if you have to ask how much yachting will set you back, you can't afford it. Polo, similarly, seems to be played only by Prince Charles and those who can stand his company for more than a few minutes at a stretch.

Basketball, on the other hand, was first played very makeshift, with a scrounged ball and a peach basket nailed to a tree. The overhead was minimal, as it still is in city playgrounds, where whole generations grow up never realizing a hoop should have a net. Many urban kids still play stickball, too, since they haven't the cash for real equipment. You don't find many people of any age in the inner city who spend their weekends on the clay courts or on the links.

Golf is the most popular sport associated with wealth, and, in one way, the most interesting, because it is both conventionally competitive and the only major sport that is ultimately, as Calhoun puts it, one of *self*-confrontation. The golfer in a tournament is involved in two tests: one against the rest of the field, the other against himself. There is even a specific measurement for his personal quest: par, the accepted level of excellence. If he either achieves or beats it, he's won; if he doesn't, he's lost—he's, by definition, a "sub-par" athlete. This is why golf has devised the handicap—if the golfer is too old, or too young, or just less gifted, he will be assigned a more realistic "par," one suited to his own level of excellence.

In a sense, golf is like baseball in this stress on individuality and in the feeling it develops in the spectator that normal folk can become mythic golfers; this may be why that, more than most sports for the wealthy, it attracts the unmonied. I myself know a poor Irishman, not particularly fond of his wealthy brethren, who both loves golf and is embarrassed by that love, and there are others like him. Despite the fact that golf's tournaments are always played at private clubs economically inaccessible to the average citizen, there remain countless municipal courses, affordable to persons of moderate means. But golf, of course, is not *just* economically defined; like other sports, it has its standard archetypal figures: Bobby Jones is conventionally Apollonian, while the high-living Walter Hagen is primarily a Dionysiac.

The Apollonian-oriented Paul Gallico, who very probably liked Hagen's company after dark, worshiped Jones in the sober daytime. The only chapter on golf in his book is called "One Hero," and it covers Jones. Gallico, writing in 1938, makes some very modern observations. He admits that, while "the sportswriter has few if any heroes," he "creates many because it is our business to do so"; then he says Jones is the exception, the man who was a hero in his individual life as well as in his mythic one. There is no evidence that Gallico was a bigot, but the possibility that Bobby Jones may have been one, a man who tried to keep blacks out of the Masters in Augusta, doesn't appear to affect his mythifying view.

If golf is a rich man's sport sometimes played by the poor, thoroughbred racing is a rich man's sport in which the poor never participate, but which they virtually support: there is no self-respecting two-dollar-window bettor who would take the day off to play 18 holes, even if it was free, when the local track was having its meeting. If golf is often played by the idle rich, Aqueduct or Arlington are just as often patronized by the idle jobless.

But is the "draw" of the track simply the need to gamble, the impulse to make a quick killing? True, you may see some of the same faces at the track that you see at the long lottery lines in the drugstore or getting off the charter bus in Atlantic City, but I believe there's something more to it than this, something else that drives the racing fan, and that it may be his deep emotional response to the horses themselves. It's this gut response to animals that makes thoroughbred racing truly unique.

Years ago, John Ruskin noted our capacity to invest dumb nature with human feelings. He called this "the pathetic fallacy," which term is still used to explain our projection of human emotions into animals, to show why we can think that the instinct of the puppy who recognizes us is not instinct but love, why we can take the snuggling of the kitten personally or why we will cry when Ruffian or Prairie Bayou has to be destroyed. The horse trainer and the vet know better—the horse does not have emotions in any human sense; even what we admire as courage or gallantry in an animal we call her or him is really something else; there can be no question of a horse's "character" or his "feelings" if the horse has neither a reasoning mind nor a soul.

That this sounds harsh is the fault of our own blindness, our denial of the fact that horses, like dogs and cats, are irrational animals. In Ruskin's phrase, we are guilty of a "pathetic fallacy" when we treat them as though they had human feelings; there is no Jonathan Livingston Whirlaway. While this doesn't alter the fact that we will all continue to make this mistake, it does help us understand our fascination with horse racing, the only major sport in which the pathetic fallacy plays a part. Certainly we ascribe humanity to other animals, and I will likely persist in believing that my dog, Frank, both admires and loves me, but we do not anthromorphize them as we do the racehorse. The difference is this: we view our pets as loving children, to be nurtured and to return our care with love; but we view horses as heroes, deifying them much as we do human athletes.

If we look at the journalistic treatment of the great thoroughbreds, Ruskin's pathetic fallacy appears everywhere. When Man o' War won the Withers at Belmont in 1920, the *New York Times* reported that, in the paddock, he had been "proud, alert, but not nervous," adding that he had, "among his many other fine qualities, a very good disposition," and that, although he was "playful when not preparing for a race," he seemed to "sense the importance" of the occasion just before post time; then he was always "anxious to get under way." When he left the paddock for the track, Man o' War was applauded "like the star of a play making his first entrance." He tugged at his bit—"but not meanly"—and, although the race was close for a while, it soon turned out that he "had only been playing with his rival." After he won, he had to stand still for a session with the photographers, this being "what all celebrities have to do" (30 May 1920: 23). Nor did this kind of description stop when Man o' War did, or even after his life: in his book of memoirs Bill Corum, who once ran Churchill Downs, speaks of him as a man and even calls him "the greatest," a label later applied to a *real* human.

The case of the great Secretariat is similar. When he won the Belmont and the Triple Crown by 31 lengths in 1973, the *Times* said he was "superequine" (10 June 1973: B12). A year later, in a book on great horses, Barbara Berry described him as one who "took things in his twenty-five-foot stride.... Far from getting nervous...he stared right back at people." She added that he had a "lovable personality," and she agreed with the *Times*, saying he was a "superhorse" (137). It was around this time that Hugh Carey, then a Representative from New York State, entered Secretariat's name into the *Congressional Record* as "Rex Americanus Equinas." Long live the first American king.

He did, although his mythical career ended in 1973. When Secretariat finally did die in 1989, the *Times* reported that he used to get "dozens of letters and birthday cards each year," claiming further that the horse had been "a shameless ham as well as a mischievous greeter" when those same fans came around to Claiborne Farms to press the fetlock (8 Oct. 1989: B25). Maybe this behavior was appropriately theatrical, since Secretariat was the only horse to have made the covers of *Time, Sports Illustrated,* and *Newsweek* simultaneously.

If reporters at least try to control their impulse to consider horses as people, often tempering their remarks with irony, private citizens needn't and don't. They can get away with writing letters and sending cards. Shortly after Secretariat was put down, Penny Chenery, a private citizen who was particularly close to Secretariat (she was his owner), wrote an article for the *New York Times*. She said:

Secretariat knew he was king of the walk, the best in the barn, and he would kind of look at Riva Ridge, his stablemate, and that look would say: "I'm the best. You're yesterday's news. They love ME."

He was a cocky horse, but not egotistical. I know it's strange to talk this way about an animal, but Secretariat was so intelligent....

He was utterly aware of his surroundings and he played to crowds.... He loved the attention. He carried himself with the same style and pride at all times....

But when he was retired to stud he became as friendly as an old puppy dog.... I saw families pose babies on his withers. Secretariat seemed to realize his role then was to be a folk hero. His demeanor was that of a champion in whatever he was asked to do....

I'm going to miss him terribly. My family and I join the many people who have been his loyal fans in great sadness at his loss. He was not only a champion race horse, but a cherished friend. (*New York Times*, 8 Oct. 1989: B25)

The above is a complete and very human biography, taking us from frisky youth through gentle old age and ending with a eulogy. All that's missing is an account of the animal's sexual prowess during the years of stud, but Ms. Chenery is a decorous person. Her account is very similar to the traditional beast fables, like those of Aesop, and it bears a particular resemblance to Chaucer's tale of the rooster Chaunticlere, a great hero who speaks perfect English.

But I do not mean to belittle our impulse to make horses so human that we truly cherish them, an impulse I certainly feel myself; can anyone watch the clip of Secretariat's Belmont without becoming emotional and dumbstruck at the same moment? Peggy Chenery explained our feelings well enough when the great horse died, but a fan at the track said it more simply. He asked why they hadn't lowered the flags at Belmont, where he was in attendance, and he was told the flags were only lowered for people. "But he wasn't a horse," the fan said; "he was *Secretariat*." The last epitaph was written by an editorial writer for the *Times*, who said, very perceptively, that Secretariat "was not a horse but the archetype of the horse," and who titled his piece *The End of Pegasus* (8 Oct. 1989: A18).

Universal Sports

Many of the sports already discussed are universal, of course—thoroughbred racing certainly is, and golf—but it seems proper to discuss them under different headings, for reasons I've already given. However, the major sport I haven't yet dealt with, boxing, could be the most universal. It is ancient, world-wide, and as basic as chess; it combines qualities of mind and body seamlessly; it even places a strong emphasis on individuality, like baseball and golf. Boxing is both brutal and destructive and a sweet science; as Joyce Carol Oates has pointed out, it's also a symbolic conflict, a drama in which the spirit tries to defeat and rise above the brute animal. In this, boxing seriously shares something with both the bullfight and Shakespeare's *The Tempest*.

Boxing's universal appeal is one reason why it is never included on any list of major American sports. While it is surely of equivalent importance here to baseball, football, or basketball, it just as surely is not solely *American*. Of course, it follows archetypal patterns just as obviously as any other sport: Dempsey is a productive Dionysiac, Tunney a conventional Apollonian, Archie Moore a trickster, and the great Ali a combination of all three; the Frazier-Ali fights pitted conservative against liberal, the Willard-Johnson fight set black against white—and the Sullivan-Corbett match dramatized the coming of age of America itself.

It's very plain that in the contrast of John L. Sullivan and James J. Corbett we are contrasting a pure Dionysiac with an Apollonian just as pure, at least in regard to their mythical lives. Even as he aged, Corbett's myth allowed him to retain the aura of the very perfect, gentle knight, even though he really was only a second-rate vaudevillian actor. When Bill Corum, for example, looked at the old fighter, he saw a man who "always exuded the gentility of his nickname...without effort or ostentation. He was ramrod straight, polite, immaculately dressed, and usually smiling...."

he was unmarked from nearly forty fights, and he spoke softly and listened considerately" (209-10).

Sullivan, on the other hand, was the cartoon of the saloon brawler, so much so that as late as 1936 Faulkner could expect his readers to know what he meant when he described a character totally incapable of learning graceful behavior:

> He was like John L. Sullivan having taught himself painfully and tediously to do the schottische, having drilled himself and drilled himself in secret until he now believed it no longer necessary to count the music's beat, say. (*Absalom, Absalom!* 46)

Sullivan, in other words, could simply never learn to dance well; dancing, and particularly around the ring, came to Corbett naturally.

When Sullivan and Corbett fought in New Orleans in September 1892, this country was just beginning the most important change in its history: it was about to grow out of its status as a rough-and-tumble frontier outpost and truly enter the international community. Sullivan, who had always fought bare-knuckle and who always drank freely during his fights, represented the old America; Corbett, a graceful boxer rather than a plodding but powerful slugger, represented the new. When Corbett's followers celebrated his victory, they were welcoming a new era; when Sullivan's fans drowned their sorrows after his loss, they were mourning the passing of an old one. But both sides must have sensed that the fight they'd just seen illustrated important changes in and for the entire country.

In other words, and despite the fact that boxing is primarily a universal sport, the Sullivan-Corbett fight is as good an example as we have of historical agon, of archetypal figures who represent different eras actually meeting in athletic combat, and, because it is such a fine example of this manifestation of sports myth, I'd like to examine it closely as an instance of a universal sports event (there was, after all, a *world* championship at stake) which also had great local significance.

Localized Universal Sport

Sullivan had one important defense before the landmark fight with Corbett, against Jake Kilrain in 1889. John L. was not in peak condition—he even vomited in the ring once—but he outlasted the over-rated Kilrain in a 75-round, three-hour marathon. When, after two years, he was attacked for not defending his title, he published his famous challenge, listing Corbett as one of his preferred opponents, and Corbett took him up on it. Most observers thought the great—the *invulnerable*—John L. would squelch his critics again.

Sullivan, probably with the help of *National Police Gazette* publisher Richard K. Fox, had made boxing by far the most popular sport in the nation, and John L. was unquestionably the country's greatest idol. In most newspapers, the Corbett fight not only took precedence over Cap Anson's Chicago Colts and the great Trotter Nancy Hanks, but also over the Lizzie Borden case and the Dalton gang's latest train robbery. The fight, properly enough, was covered more extensively than the death of John Greenleaf Whittier, but it also proved bigger news than the presidential election. Recognizing the irony of this, *The New York World* ran a cartoon captioned "The Overshadowing Issue of the Week" in which Corbett and Sullivan were shown casting a large shadow over the much smaller figures of Harrison and Cleveland (2 Sep. 1892: 21).

The World was right. Sullivan, in particular, was more important than the President to most Americans. Look at the newspaper accounts of Sullivan's two-day trip from Brooklyn to New Orleans and you'll see what *The World* meant.

The Dionysiac Brawler

On Thursday, September 1, six days before the fight, Sullivan went through a final workout at Phil Casey's Brooklyn Handball Club. Admiring bystanders counted as he jumped rope 784 times, got a rubdown and then, ten minutes later, jumped rope 714 times more. He was weighed and he clocked in at 209. Since he had been accused of being fat, onlookers were encouraged both to look at the scales and to adjust the weights themselves, and about a dozen people took advantage of the offer.

About 10 a.m. Sullivan started for the Holmes Street Theatre, where he rehearsed the third act of *Honest Hearts and Willing Hands* for two hours and then had a big meal, topped off with a bottle of Bass ale. A few minutes before 3 in the afternoon he left the club with Casey and Mayor John Carmody. The crowd outside pressed in, and two cops had to be called over before he was able to move. The people sent up three rousing cheers for "John L. Sullivan, the champion of the world," and the big fellow took off his hat and said, "Thank you, boys."

Sullivan's party left in hacks. One pretty little woman put her hand on the Boston man for just a second and then hurried away, seemingly proud that she had touched the Sullivan arm, and John L. grinned. When they got to Charley Johnston's restaurant, another great crowd was waiting, but Sullivan was able to get past them and into a private room, where he stayed until about 4, when the party left again. The cabs took them across the Brooklyn Bridge, which was also crowded with well-wishers.

There was a large crowd in front of Jimmy Wakely's place at 6th Avenue and 42nd Street, as it was thought Sullivan would take the midtown crossing, but he was driven instead to the Jay Street ferry on West 13th and got over to the West Shore Railroad station in Weehawken from there. At the station he was driven directly to his private car, the Blithedale. The crowd there was clamoring for him, and just before the train left at 5:30 he came out on the rear platform of his coach, bowed, and as the crowd surged toward him said he was theirs very truly, John L. Sullivan, and that he would return to New York as World's Champion. They cheered, and the cheering continued as the train pulled out. As it picked up steam a close friend of the champion called him aside and asked: "Now, John, do you really think you can win?"

"Win, win!" he asked in surprise. "Now how can I lose! Why, I'll punch holes in that bank clerk. Who ever heard of a counter jumper that could fight! A draw! I guess not. I'll give handsome Jimmy one of the best lickings he ever got in his life. I'll finish him in short order, too, and don't you forget it. I'll teach him a lesson he'll remember for many days to come. Won't I, sport?" and he slapped his trainer good-naturedly on the back.

The Sullivan special, well-stocked with whiskey and wine and with an even dozen broiled chickens cooked especially for John L. by Jimmy Wakely's wife, six chickens for each day on the road, headed up through New York State. Aboard, in addition to Casey, Johnston and Wakely, were Sullivan's brawny handler and look-alike, Liney Tracy, and Billy Pond, his Japanese valet, whom everybody called simply "The Jap." At Coeyman's Junction, near Albany, the village band, which had walked a mile to get there, serenaded Sullivan with more noise than music, and there were cries of "Sullivan, put in your best licks!" and "Jack, we are with you!" A little later the big fellow went off to bed, singing, "If you want to git to heaven on de nickel plated road / Just push dem clouds away." At one in the morning the train passed through Utica, and at about two the lights of Syracuse could be seen and the engineer blew a long blast on his whistle. Twenty-five diehards were on the platform hoping to see Sullivan. When the train reached Rochester at 4 a.m. only a few fans were there to greet it.

By the time the train pulled into Buffalo at dawn, an impressed porter had cleaned up almost two bushels of empty bottles, corks, bits of bread, chunks of meat, and cigar boxes, and Sullivan was going from berth to berth, playfully poking in the ribs those pals who were awake. At Dunkirk, at 8:30, John L. was given his breakfast, and there was the usual crowd and a band to give him a morning tune. The train moved on into Pennsylvania, and at the Erie stop nearly everybody piled off to eat a mass breakfast that had been arranged beforehand. Once the train got to Ohio it was discovered that the drunken Steve Brodie, who had for some reason debarked in Buffalo, had forgotten to get back on, and a great sigh of relief went up.

At Cleveland several hundred men peered through the iron railing and yelled for the champion until he showed himself, tipped his cap, bowed, and returned to his car. At Crestline seven-year-old May Colvin gave the fighter a bouquet with a card reading, "to John L. Sullivan, the champion of the world." She told him her mamma had asked her to present him with the flowers, and her visit left him in a serious mood. At Springfield 300 people cheered until Sullivan came out, and as he pulled off his cap with a jerk, showing his closely cropped head, they yelled again and louder, and someone said he was "the stuff." At Dayton the Mayor sent in his card and was briefly received. "Mr. Sullivan," he said, "I am indeed glad of an opportunity of meeting such a representative American as you are."

At Cincinnati, however, the crowd was overwhelming. *The New York World* estimated it at 10,000. The terminal was entirely filled with people. Small boys hung on the pilasters and perched on the guard fences, and a detail of fifty cops had a hard time keeping order. The doors to John L.'s car had to be locked to protect him from the swarms of fans who leaped onto the platform and clung to the rails. Finally Liney Tracy was sent out in a white sweater and cap to impersonate the champ. A howl went up as he reached the platform, and when, in a deep, guttural voice, he growled, "How de do, boys," the crowd went into ecstasies.

Now the train turned south. Just before Chattanooga, where Charley Johnston was wanted by the law in connection with a previous fight illegally held in Tennessee, the Sullivan special was split. The Blithedale, with Johnston aboard, was sidetracked and drawn quietly through the back of the yard while the rest of the train stopped at the station to be welcomed by the usual tumultuous crowd. After it got safely past Chattanooga, the engine pulling the Blithedale put on a full head of steam and didn't stop until it was safely in Morganville, just across the line in Georgia, where it waited for the rest of the special.

That morning John L. got up at dawn and worked out with Casey. He hadn't shaved since leaving Brooklyn, and he sported an eight-inch, two-day, blue-black stubble. In the afternoon, to give the people along the route a chance to see him, he stood outside on the rear platform of the Blithedale, and at Birmingham another mob of 10,000 took the day off from work to see the champ, yelling "Put him to sleep!" and "Blow his ears off!"

At 2 a.m. the next day the train pulled into Richburg, Mississippi, where the people had lit bonfires. With the help of these, plus the light of the full moon, John L. was able to recognize the site of his fight with Kilrain, so he woke up Phil Casey to tell him where the ring had been and to explain how he had made his way to it. A crowd of a hundred or so blacks repeatedly called for him to show himself, but Sullivan was tired and went back to his berth. Then four men came forward to serenade the champ, for some reason picking a totally inappropriate popular song called "Down on the Farm." They were so bad that some of the party reached quickly for the bottle, while John L. himself buried his head in his pillows, saying, "I don't know what I've done to deserve this," but adding that he didn't want to hurt those fellows' feelings. They kept it up. "For goodness' sake, how much longer do we stop here?" said Sullivan, and when the train finally started up again he heaved a sigh of relief and went to sleep.

In New Orleans, a rumor had spread that the train was heading for the Louisville & Nashville depot at the head of Canal Street, so 4,000 or 5,000 fans gathered there, but it went instead to the Northeastern terminal on the north side of the Quarter. It moved slowly up to the platform at 5 a.m., the lights of Algiers on the left and the sheds of the French Market on the right. The buildings of the city stood out gray against the gray dawn sky. To the south, threatening clouds were forming.

When John L. got off, he was wearing a black sweater, dark pants and a black silk cap with a peak. Because most people thought he was arriving at the station across town, the crowd was manageable, and he was able to get away without much difficulty. He was taken straight to his room. For some reason, his hack passed Mrs. Green's at 29 North Rampart, even though he had stayed with her before the Kilrain fight and she had reserved rooms for his entire party, and went on to Mrs. Hamilton's, at number 45. The champion went straight to bed, despite the crowd which was already outside clamoring for him.

The crowd dispersed briefly around noon when the storm clouds broke, but after the shower they were back, and when John L. went across the street in the afternoon to work out at the Young Men's Gymnasium Club the police had to clear a path with what the Chicago Tribune called "a systematic course of clubbing." After this, John L. decided he'd had enough of his public, and the next day he moved with his party across Canal to the St. Charles Hotel. At least here he had a choice of exits.

The Field of Battle

New Orleans was packed with fight fans. Lem Felcher had come down from Toronto wearing a heavy double-gold watch chain, a locket encrusted with enormous diamonds with a scarfpin to match, diamond cufflinks and gold rings on every finger. Lem was a Sullivan man. When the so-called Whiskey Unlimited arrived from Chicago it disgorged, among others, a man named Sport Campana. Sport had had John L.'s head and shoulders tattooed on his chest just before leaving for the fight.

There were familiar names, too. In the St. Charles' lobby the reporter for *The New York Sun* ran into a pleasant man with big blue eyes and a trustful, frank expression, and wondered how people could think he was dangerous; this was Bat Masterson, who was betting $250 that Corbett would take Sullivan in 20 rounds. One-Eyed Connelly was also a Corbett man, although Steve Brodie was solidly for Sullivan. Connelly and Brodie didn't get along in any case, but their different preferences on this occasion could only make matters worse. They finally ran into each other on Labor Day in the bar at the St. Charles. Brodie had just found a "sucker" who was willing to put $200 on Corbett and he was celebrating by opening a quart bottle for his friends. One of those friends playfully asked Connelly to have a glass.

"You'll have to excuse me," Connelly said. "I wouldn't drink with him if I never took a drink."

"No, and I wouldn't ask the likes of you to take a drink, anyhow," snarled Brodie. "I don't wish to associate with you at all, Mr. Connelly, and if you attempt to speak to me on the streets of New Orleans I shall call an officer and have you thrown into the cooler, where you belong."

This set the blood of the Bostonian boiling, and he spluttered around for nearly a minute before he could say anything. "There's one thing about it," he finally exclaimed. "I'm on the level, I am, and I don't go around throwing dummies off bridges and claiming I jumped off."

"I'll bet you $5,000 I never threw a dummy off a bridge," retorted Brodie. "But if I ever catch you on a bridge I'll throw you off. You'll answer first-rate for a dummy, and it wouldn't take me long to fire you into the river."

Mutual friends intervened and a bloody battle was averted.

In the meantime Corbett, and nemesis, had slipped in relative quiet into town.

Single Combat

The Olympic Club stood ten blocks north of the French Quarter, between Montegut, Clouett, Royal, and Chartres. Inside there were luxuriously furnished parlors, a fine billiard hall, a café, card rooms and, in the central yard area and under a removable tarpaulin roof, the arena. A 24-foot ring surrounded a fighting surface of tightly packed Mississippi sand, and around this ring, about six feet further out, was another ring of barbed wire. Ringside seats and boxes were positioned just beyond the barbed wire ring.

The fight itself was described at length and in detail in all the papers, but the most interesting account may have been the most authentic. With an eye toward publishing a pamphlet afterwards, Prof. James Connors, boxing instructor at the Buffalo Athletic Club, brought two dummies to ringside. It's not recorded whether or not he paid for three seats, but when a punch was thrown by either boxer he marked the appropriate dummy at the precise anatomical point where that punch landed, and if the punch had been what he called a "staggering hit" he marked it with a Maltese cross. The account that resulted showed a fight that followed the common pattern in which an older man is worn down by a younger.

In Round 1 (and all the other accounts agree on this) neither fighter landed a punch of any kind. The first "staggering hit" occurred in Round 5, and it was Corbett who threw it; it landed flush on Sullivan's nose. In Round 7

Corbett connected solidly again. In both Round 9 and Round 11 he landed two "staggering hits," and he hit Sullivan hard three times in Round 15.

The fight, the title, and the era were slipping away. In Round 15 a desperate Sullivan connected with his first good punch, hitting Corbett over the heart. In the 16th he caught Corbett on the chin, but not only was Jim unhurt, he answered John L. with two good shots of his own, one to the belly and one underneath the left eye. Both fighters took it easy in Round 17, but in the 18th Corbett went back to the attack and caught Sullivan twice, once to the right of the nose and once on the chin.

In the 19th Sullivan landed one last good blow, but after that it was virtually all over. An exhausted John L. could manage only a total of four weak punches, none classed as "staggering hits" by Connors, for the rest of the fight. In Round 20 Corbett caught Sullivan well twice; in Round 21 Corbett caught him three times, once in the belly, once on the cheek and, finally, once on the chin. After the last good punch Sullivan fell to the canvas, rolled over on his stomach, and was counted out. Corbett threw a total of 25 punches in that final round; Sullivan threw none.

The Dionysiac in Defeat

As Sullivan lay on the canvas, Corbett, in the center of the ring, raised his arms in victory and then jumped through the ropes, shaking hands with friends on the other side of the barbed wire. Sullivan, who had been helped to his corner, gradually came to, and after he did he walked unsteadily back into the ring and held on to the top rope.

"Ladies and gentlemen," he said, "it is the old, old story. The story of a young man against an old one. There are gray hairs in my head and I should have known better. I can only say that I am glad that the championship is to remain in America. That is all I've got say." Then he walked back to his corner and sat down again on his stool.

Back in the locker room, a doctor put three stitches in Sullivan's split nose. The fighter already had a glass of wine in his hand, and he was crying.

"I'm sorry about my friends losing their money," he said to Charley Johnston. Johnston told him not to worry, that his friends were his friends and would remain loyal.

When the Sullivan party got back to the St. Charles it was already 2 a.m. Sullivan ordered the doors locked, and the only person allowed in was the young bellboy, who at one point said, "Gee, but those fellows drink a heap," and reported they were all drinking ale "by the bottle." At 3 a.m. Sullivan and two friends left for the bars, and at 4:30 they were seen coming back, very drunk. They staggered upstairs and re-enlisted the bellboy until 5, when John L. loudly announced he was going to retire. He had to be undressed and led to his bed, where he passed out in a pile of pillows.

The next morning Sullivan got up at 11. He dressed and tried to eat, but found he couldn't chew even the pear, let alone the broiled chicken or the mutton chop he'd been served. He could drink, though, and starting at noon he began. He held a pitcher in one hand; the Jap would open two bottles of ale, pour them in the pitcher and John L. would drain it. By 1 he had finished eight pitchers.

When he left the hotel for his evening train back north there were not twenty people to see John L. Sullivan off, although at the depot there were perhaps a hundred. He got on the train, started drinking beer, and eventually went to sleep drunk. The next day the train passed through Akron. Twenty or thirty black laborers stared at the train and at Sullivan's battered face in the window. Nobody cheered.

The Victorious Apollonian

After the fight the new champion went with his party to a reception at the Southern Athletic Club, where he was cheered by 2,000 people. Bottles of champagne were popped open all around, but the champion declined. "Milk is good enough for me," he said, and raised a glass of milk to his mouth. One of his friends, who hadn't had a drop for two years, proposed a champagne toast. "Wait a minute," Corbett said. "You can drink my health in water, but if you touch that wine to your lips I will never speak to you again. I won't have your pledge broken for my sake." Then he was given a telegram from his wife which read: "Bless your heart. We were not overconfident, were we?—Ollie." Ollie, who had heard of Sullivan's concession speech, had previously told a reporter, "Wasn't that nice of Mr. Sullivan to say what he did?"

The next day Corbett went to the Grand Opera House, where he had a role in a play called *After Dark*. It was pandemonium when he appeared. Ladies applauded and waved their handkerchiefs; men pounded the ferules from their canes and broke their umbrellas, and men and boys burst into long, loud cheering. Shouting itself hoarse the audience at last became quiet and Corbett said:

> I am not a speaker, and I have no speech to make. All I can say is that I will ever have a soft spot in my heart for this city. Here I started upon my career, and here I reached the top of the ladder. I can not tell you how I appreciate what New Orleans has done for me and how I have been treated.

Then the cheering broke forth again and continued for a long time. But finally the play went on, and ended, and after many curtain calls and hearty good-byes the champion was almost alone and ready to leave early the next morning. Just as he was preparing to leave New Orleans, perhaps the only man that weekend to do so dead sober, his mother was being interviewed by a reporter back home in San Francisco:

> "Well, I am glad he beat Sullivan," she said, "and I am glad he is safe. I have had eleven children and ten of them are living, but Jim was always my favorite. I was always proud of him because he was a good-looking lad, and he has always been so good to me. No mother ever had a better son. He always obeyed me and was never vicious. I don't like prize fighting, but I must say I don't believe a successful fighter must be a brutal man, for I know Jimmy is not of that nature. There never was a kinder hearted boy than he."

A milk-drinking, mannerly man with an ideal mom and a wife out of Jane Austen was the new heavyweight champ.

No wonder Sullivan was driven to drink. But even though John L.'s supporters still couldn't believe the tragedy that had befallen them, there was a great amount of rejoicing among the Corbett fanciers, who seemed more aware than the Sullivanites of the significance of the fight. *The San Francisco Examiner*, for example, interviewed a man of the cloth who wanted Corbett to win because he set a better example, while noting that Sullivan was still picked by what they called "the poolroom element." And *The New York Times* ran an editorial after Corbett's victory in which they analyzed the "extraordinary interest" in the fight:

> For a decade or more SULLIVAN has been swaggering about as an unconquerable person, and he is the embodiment of everything that is loathsome in the professional pugilist.... SULLIVAN is a malignant brute who has regarded every man who aspired to beat him as a personal enemy, and has thereby made everybody who has followed his career, or upon whose attention his career has been forced, yearn to see somebody give him an exemplary thrashing.... the dethronement of a mean and cowardly bully as the idol of the barrooms is a public good that is a fit subject for public congratulation. (8 Sep. 1892: 19)

Clearly the Sullivan-Corbett fight had been something more than a battle between two individuals.

The Fight as Historical Agon

According to historian Elliott Gorn, John L. Sullivan was "the most idolized athlete of the entire nineteenth century" (216). Randy Roberts calls him "the most popular fighter of all time" (101), and suggests that this is because the people felt he represented America itself: if Sullivan was the greatest fighter in the world, and if Sullivan was an American, then America must be the greatest country in the world (17-18). John D. McCallum said Sullivan was thought of as "the hero of the Gaslight Era" (4) and that he "fitted the time perfectly" and "belonged in the rough, raw America of his day" (20). Gorn, speaking of "the champion's legendary conviviality, his embrace of the easy camaraderie of saloons and sporting houses," also stressed the symbolic value of his persona:

> John L. loved the good life, including elegant clothes, expensive jewelry, the finest foods, the best cigars, and free-flowing champagne. Everyone knew of his drinking binges and his extramarital affairs. Everyone also knew of the gorgeous barroom he opened in Boston to treat and toast his friends. He embodied Gilded Age fascination with rich living and gaudy displays of wealth. (225)

Rex Lardner said Sullivan "epitomized a nation beginning to feel its muscles" (57), and he added this:

> Brawling, rowdy, robust America—with its Manifest Destiny, free enterprise and good fellowship enhanced by bad whiskey; Conestogas fording rivers and hurtling down hills; vast waterways being dug to link lakes and rivers; rails being laid down by coolies moving east and by Irish immigrants moving west—seemed to be epitomized by the personality, in the ring and out, of the swaggering, supremely confident, never-take-a-back-step Boston Strong Boy. (43)

Considering all this it is hardly surprising that, as John Durant said, when Corbett KO'd Sullivan he "committed the unforgiveable [sic] sin of deposing a national idol" (37).

Still, the future, as well as the day, was Corbett's, because he represented the emerging America as surely as Sullivan did the passing era. Corbett, who was vain about his nickname and "obsessed with his own urbanity" (McCallum 28), "brought class to the prize ring.... A polished, cultured man, he proved to the world that good fighters did not necessarily have to be loutish ignoramuses or hoodlums to succeed" (22). Corbett even reported in his autobiography that he was "disgusted" with the crowd that cheered him when Sullivan went down, presumably because of their ungentlemanly shifting of allegiance (20).

The passing of the championship belt from Sullivan to Corbett paralleled the change in the national mood in several important ways. The most obvious shift, as the *New York Times* editorial suggests, was ethical. A brawling drunk, an emblem of mindlessness and brute power, could no longer be tolerated as a national symbol. His replacement drank infrequently or not at all, and he was polite and courteous to a fault, but he was no less a powerful hero for all that. Although it was difficult for the country to let go, to finally turn its back on the spirit of the rugged settler who had made a place for himself out of sheer strength, the time had come. The new hero had to represent a new spirit, one of consolidation after the frontiers had been closed. After conquest and settlement comes civilization.

Americans wanted boxing to be both more humane and more refined, since they were beginning to cultivate those qualities in themselves. When the game was changed and the Queensbury Rules superseded those of Broughton and the London Prize Ring, they got what they wanted, and all that was needed now was a new hero to fit this new game. Sullivan was inappropriate for that role, but Corbett played it so well that his victory almost seems more a matter of the inevitable flow of history than of one individual's youth and skill. The frontier was gone; the next territory to be conquered would be Spanish, and the country as a whole was looking to Europe and to America's entrance into the international community as a major power. The country was growing up, for better or for worse, as the continental Americans of Henry James began to take over Huck Finn's territory in the national imagination. Strong Boy had given way to Gentle Man. Still, with most gain there is some concurrent loss. John Barrymore remembered an incident which occurred not long after the great fight. John McCallum describes it:

> Barrymore was in his early teens by this time, and had made a date to meet his father on Broadway. As the two Barrymores stood there a bulking man walked slowly past them. A quality of loneliness seemed upon him in this busy street. The elder Barrymore took a quick step toward the big man, calling out cordially, "Hello there, John!"
>
> John L. Sullivan paused, turned his great head slowly, as if he suspected some kind of mischief. Suddenly

his eye fired with recognition. "Aw, Barry! It's you. Guess I was just all wrapped in myself too hard. Nice of you to speak to me."

The ex-hero resumed his gallant march down Broadway, the ghosts of former worshippers following his slow strides. (20)

The Great John L. America no longer had any use for him; it had adopted new ways, and taken to heart a new personification of those ways. The Great John L. He had lost his symbolic value, and so had become just another ex-pug surprised when somebody recognized him on the street. When John Sullivan, the plain citizen, walked down Broadway that day, he was on his way out of the consciousness of the country, and he knew it.

Chapter 13

THE PRESS

> The history of baseball is a lie from beginning to
> end.... all of it is bunk, tossed up with a wink and a
> nudge.
>
> —John Thorn
> ("The Father of Baseball?" 85)

Likewise the histories of football, and basketball, and
boxing, and every other sport, because all sports force second
identities onto players, force real individuals to wear the
archetypal uniforms that are always hanging in the lockers
of myth. While once in a while the individual himself will
encourage the transformation by believing what he has heard
for years and has at last forgotten to be false, usually the
fault is ours: the fans and their representatives, the writers
and sportscasters, are the responsible parties. I've mentioned
Jim Brosnan's name for the real fan, the one who is a fanatic
in nearly the literal sense; it's the "Inner Fan," a man who
"will create players in his own image—a man making gods."
The Inner Fan, Brosnan says, has a "single-minded desire to
seek absolute identification with the player" (638-40). Cozens
and Stumpf come to a similar conclusion when they say the
fan has a "need for vicarious personal contacts...which would
permit him the illusion of sharing an emotional experience,"
and they add the figure of the "sports writer" who must both
"experience the thrills [of the sport] and understand the
enthusiasm of its devotees" (115-16): their "writer" in other
words is a middle figure, both vicarious participant and
historian. And so the obvious question, the rub: can a
participant of any kind ever be an objective observer? While
there may be some writers over the years who have been
completely fair, they have probably been few. The reason
baseball's Hall of Fame at Cooperstown is an institution of

139

dubious standards is that the writers, personally involved, are asked to set those standards. And does anyone really think that the writer who gave Ted Williams no MVP votes in 1941 was more cold-eyed observer than passionate (if misguided) fan?

Writers, in fact, are our messengers; while they do occasionally try to inform and instruct us, they are much more likely to reflect our own ideas. This is how archetypal figures are made. The writers, who have access to the athletes as real individuals, judge them in the time-honored way, by deciding which archetypal costume fits each one best; then we are told their decision—which probably would have been ours, too. So I think that the sociologists Cramer, Walker, and Rado are clearly right when they say "the values and interests of the reporter" are vital to the image of the athlete that reporter creates, although their finding that "sportswriters are influenced by their perceptions of what their readers want" is less sure (175, 181), and may just reflect the wish of the writers they interviewed to be considered good business people. After all, the job of the sports journalist usually hinges more on his style (verbal or oratorical) than on whether the public agrees with his pronouncements; anyhow, it's more likely that the journalist and the fan will agree, because they are both fans in the first place, because their judgments tend naturally to gibe.

The final element in the role of fan and writer in creating myth is, obviously, the Olympus of archetypes, the pantheon of god-heroes that hovers over every element of this study. The archetypes, as always, being permanent patterns in the human psyche, come first; then come the individual athletes, ripe for the mythifying. Since the rest of us virtually never come into close contact with these figures as real humans, we rely on our messengers, the journalists, to know them; the journalists then send us the news. This system differs little from that used in the classical era, when oracles and bards told us about the gods and, even if it seems odd to imagine Howard Cosell in a cave, it's nonetheless true that an awareness of this system will inevitably help elucidate any myth made by humans.

SUMMARY OUTLINES

The Archetypal Journey

VALHALLA

(Sages, Strongmen, and Martyrs)

ARCADIA → Separation → Test → Return → UTOPIA

UNDERWORLD

(Fools, Failures, and Pariahs)

The individual's *real* life extends from Arcadia well beyond Utopia (his successful playing years).

The climax of the individual's quest is a *test*, during which he must prove either his physical or his mental superiority, or both. If he passes, he gains Utopia, which, as the mature realization of the innocent Arcadian dream, represents a return to a land that's paradise, only better.

The individual's *mythic* life is not recorded until he leaves Arcadia and begins his quest for Utopia, and even then it may never be recorded (few minor-league baseball players are remembered, however brilliant their careers). Even the athlete who enters Utopia for a year or two may never be given a mythic life. Practically speaking, the individual's mythic history is normally chronicled only after he's not only entered Utopia, but also seems likely to stay there. This means that a large part of his quest—everything from the Arcadian beginnings to the initial achievement of the Utopian goal—will have to be set down in retrospect, a fact which in no way inhibits his chronicler's natural inventive powers.

After the individual's earthly mythic life ends in withdrawal from his game, his supernatural life (like his real one) may continue, if he's been relegated to either Valhalla or to the Underworld.

Any successful athlete has at least two lives, his real and biological life and his mythic one, and particular fame can bring him a third, the supernatural life. The mythic life ends first, then the real one, unless he is martyred; the supernatural life goes on forever.

The Archetypal Figures
(with their divisions)

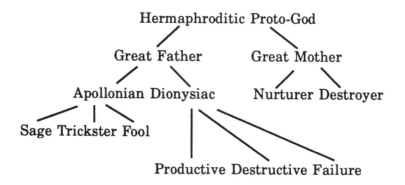

The most comprehensive archetypes (proto-god, great father, and great mother) are generally too broad to be useful in a study like this; in other words, we seldom find individuals grand enough to fill these slots. Nearly all athlete-heroes are from the third and fourth levels, and especially from Apollonian and Dionysiac and their subsidiary varieties.

Any individual may (and often does) fill more than one archetypal "slot," although most individuals, however many-sided they may be *as* individuals, are given a primary identity as a manifestation of just one.

There are potentially an infinite number of archetypes. I have tried to simplify rather than complicate this study by restricting myself to a minimum.

Variants of the Archetypal Figures

These are always figures who represent variations on the norm of the monomyth and its components. "Norm" here can mean a fully completed journey, or an archetypal figure who is healthy and mature (neither very young nor very old), or a figure who remains true to the colors of his character, like Achilles or Babe Ruth, never either changing or pretending to.

Atypical Journeys
Martyr
Pariah
Atypical Figures
Youth
Age
Altered Figures
Role-Changers
Mask-Wearers

IV. The Agonistic Archetypes

Hero
& → Ri✗al → Goal → Receiver
Helper

Judge

Of these six archetypes taken from Souriau, the only one peripheral to the action/agon is the judge, so the above is a reasonably legitimate schema of archetypal conflict. The center of any agon is this: the hero and the helper must conquer the hero of the opposing pantheon (our side calls him a *rival*) in order to attain the goal and present it to the receiver. Note that the agonistic pattern is very much like that of the archetypal journey, although it has more of a social or selfless emphasis; if the archetypal hero's quest is to pass a test and "create" *himself*, becoming a legitimate demigod, the agonistic hero is fighting for his *people*, or his team. Social concern is the center of most conflict-centered myth: Achilles, helped by Athene, defeats Hector, and is chiefly responsible for gaining Troy and Helen, which goals are then received by Agamemnon and Menelaus, respectively; Adam, helped by Eve, beats the devil, gaining salvation for all mankind. Judges watch over these actions, too: in the *Iliad*, there is Zeus, reluctant to condemn Hector, but even-handed after consulting his golden scales; in *Paradise Lost*, of course, the judge is God Himself.

The distinction between the archetypal journey and the agonistic myth has particular bearing on athletes when we recognize it does separate the self-serving from the personally ambitious, and that is just to say this: team players are vitally involved in the agon; hot dogs are only interested in the hero's quest.

Although we are all aware that some athlete-heroes are primarily selfless, some largely selfish, it's very possible to have a hero who has it both ways, fulfilling his own hero's destiny while fighting unrelentingly for his team. Such a mythic man, whatever else you may think of him, was Pete Rose, but Rose is only one of thousands of happy examples we may take from every sport. The following grid shows how athletes might be placed both according to their archetypal "slots" and according to their functions in the group-oriented agon (I've omitted "goal" and "judge" as irrelevant to the athlete's mythical persona). I leave the spaces blank; the rest, dear reader, is up to you.

		Hero	Rival	Helper	Receiver
Apollonians	Sage				
	Trickster				
	Fool				
Dionysiacs	Productive				
	Destructive				
	Failure				
Nurturers					
Destroyers					

I have included no charts on archetypal tools or archetypal location because those concepts should not be troublesome enough to require any further clarification.

EPILOGUE:
BASEBALL AND THE FANS

> What is the "best" illusion under which to live? Or,
> what is the most legitimate foolishness?
>
> —Ernest Becker
> (*The Denial of Death* 202)

So far I've discussed how humans take reality and revise it by forcing it into archetypes, or how history becomes myth; now I'd like to ask what value that myth has, if any, for the mythifiers, the fans who created it in the first place. By now it's obvious that there's little factual truth in the story of baseball, that it's all bunk, as Thorn says, or illusory, as Becker would have it. Nonetheless, a lot of national energy went into its creation. Is there anything important to it?

First we'd better take a look at our peculiar history. This country began as a neglected child who ended up a runaway, in the process cutting off all ties with the home we knew, and it seems to me that this has left an indelible mark on the American psyche, which psyche ever since has lacked the double anchors of parent and home. Isn't it significant that Britain has never felt the need to call King Alfred anything but "the Great," while we must think of George Washington as "the father of our country," and of his partners in rebellion as "the founding fathers"? And about a hundred years later, the industrial revolution compounded the problem; as America moved from a nation of self-employed individuals (80 percent in 1800) to a nation of employees (67 percent in 1870), the commitment of the American to his work and his working life decreased in its intensity, and what Thomas Greenfield called "a loosening of the work ethic" (7) developed; once an individual no longer sells what he produces, that is, no longer owns his shop or farm, but merely sells his labor to another (that is, to an employer) he not only becomes alienated from his work, he spends much less time in the home. The son of David Leverenz's "vanished father" grows up in what he feels is a fatherless house (271).

It's no accident that *Roots* was the highest-rated show in U.S. television history at the time of its showing, and blacks were by no means the only members of that very American audience. The feeling here in 1776 must have been similar to what the Bounty mutineers felt on Christmas Island: the family had been lost, the home as well, and the new land in which they wandered, somewhere east of Eden, was all that was left. Like those mutineers, the Americans had to start from scratch.

And when they started working, what did they build? The Americans of 1776 were men of the Enlightenment, some of that reasonable period's greatest minds. They formed a system of government more nearly Utopian than any yet seen, and since their faith tended more toward rational deism than Methodistical excess, you can legitimately say there was a kind of secularization of conventional religion, the sacred texts becoming the Constitution and the Declaration, the sacred temple, the Supreme Court. This capacity to make, not only a new society, but a new faith, what historians call a civil religion, has important ramifications for the American attitude toward baseball, since we really have taken a simple game and made it holy ritual.

At the time of the American Revolution, then, the national psyche had voluntarily placed itself in a difficult or even untenable position. It had rejected its father-figure and left home for good; it had even, in creating a new social system, left its old church. Its search for replacements for these things would never be completely fulfilled; as a result, the unsatisfied yearning for parent, home, and faith is always evident in most aspects of American life. When rounders became popular in the U.S. around 1820, these lacks began to become manifest in the way Americans responded to the ball-and-stick game.

Let's start with the absent father. So much has been written in America about the emotional bond between father and son as they stand before the sunny shrine of baseball that even to bring it up again is trite. Donald Hall talks about playing catch with his son, W.P. Kinsella about playing catch with his father, the seraphic Roger Angell discusses his baseball bonding with both; Warren Goldstein suggests that sons use baseball as a medium for communicating, because baseball "is one of the few sanctional vocabularies with which we can talk to our fathers" (27). While certainly the reflections of these writers demonstrate continuity, the persistence of baseball through the generations, I would argue that the emphasis is never on the son, but always on the father, the absent father. Hall is much more powerful when he writes about the young father he never knew than when he writes about his son; Angell's portrait of his old man reminiscing about Terry Turner and Nap Lajoie is the finest piece ever by a very fine writer, and much superior to his comparatively offhand concern about his own ten-year-old's reaction to his first game. As far as the power of Kinsella's myth, what American hasn't choked at the scene in the movie version when Kevin Costner's dead father appears on screen, suddenly and without warning, as a relaxed and healthy young ballplayer? As these and other writers illustrate, even when the focus appears to be on the child, this is illusory; the writer is really looking back to his own childhood, depicting himself as a child watching his own father, who is usually dead, and therefore most emphatically absent. In Goldstein's perceptive phrase, the myth of baseball offers sons "the tantalizing possibility of a filial homecoming" (27).

The most sentimental cliché in baseball theory has to do with "home," the word, the concept, and the base. Because it's a cliché, however, doesn't mean it's invalid. It runs something like this: baseball is the most pastoral of sports, steeped in the tradition of Sir Thomas More and Sir Philip Sidney, and founded on the yearning for a regained and improved paradise (what I call Utopia), all of this reflected by the chief purpose of the game, which is to get "safely home." This analysis is fine, as far as it goes, although it falls down in one vital respect; the American, perpetual yearner, never does get all the way home, even if his team has won in a rout.

Think first of the history of the U.S., and "home" in the physical sense, the sense of place. America has always been a country of expansion, of a frontier that moved regularly west. As a result, it's always been a country of migration, of settlers, of physical rootlessness. You can find this particularly in the great myths of nineteenth-century American fiction, all of which involve restless tramping or riding or boating, in books like *Moby-Dick*, *The Prairie*, and *Huck Finn*. There seems never any hope of any American's gaining a physical "home"; everything's simply too new, and, as Sartre pointed out, as soon as we put up a building, we tear it down again anyway. Well, if we can't have a home that's physically localized, possibly there could be another kind of "home" for Americans, more of a spiritual one, maybe even a "home" partaking of the mystical and the changeless. Maybe Wordsworth's world is too much with us. Possibly we need the perfection, stability, and agelessness of Coleridge's Xanadu—or of Wrigley Field.

We could be getting closer to a truth here. Romanticism was also born in the Enlightenment, and it also became a secular religion which men could use in lieu of orthodox faith. Think of the three novels I just mentioned: in each, the hero is closely bonded with another male, and in every case the male is older, and in every case the older male comes from a primitive culture: Ishmael has the Polynesian cannibal Queequeg, Natty has the Mohican Chingachgook, and Huck has the African Jim. These three primitive men— "natural" men is a better term—all have primitive faiths, and all three men are taken quite seriously, both by their partners and by their creators, as possessors of an irrational but essential wisdom. They are elemental, all three; but if they represent the heart of darkness, then the darkness is good, and the path down which they will lead their American disciples, or sons, may indeed be the path to salvation. Here we are in the realm of Rousseau, not of Thomas Hobbes. True, neither Cooper's novel nor Melville's ends with much positive achievement, but Huck, as he says, "lights out for the territory," an emotional territory that only the most hidebound rationalist could call imaginary.

Let me try to put all this back into the context of baseball. If you reach "home" or get a "home run" in the merely physical sense, you're still only talking about a game, and rounders has not yet been transfigured by American myth-makers; if your notion of "home" has more to do with the sudden clutch you feel at your throat when you walk up out of the darkness into the bleachers at Fenway Park on a bright day, then you're lighting out for the territory.

American baseball, which helps Americans find fathers and roots, is certainly a faith, if a secularized one. The great round ballparks really are cathedrals; the ceremony does remain the same, no matter who officiates, and in the magic circle of the playing area that ceremony will tease you out of thought, as doth eternity. A green baseball field on a sunny summer's day is as changelessly fixed as a vision by Blake, and as true.

I am not being frivolous in comparing the experience of American baseball to the vision of the Romantics: watching the baseball hero achieve Utopia involves the watcher in his own ecstatic return, irrational but imaginative and true, to a perfected Garden. It is not at all silly to say that in the tranquility of this game you recollect past emotions, which then create in you spontaneous and powerful feeling.

When we realize how fundamentally baseball helps satisfy yearnings which are particularly American, we should see why it's so important to us. The American ballpark is a place, not of escape, but of epiphany, and it's been made that way by the collective emotional effort of a nation. The old and unchanging ball game represents a return to a now-perfected paradise that is real, not illusory; we've gone to a place where we can find our fathers, our roots, and something to believe in; it's the place of the first game, the game that is still going on, where, as Angell says, that ball that was tossed in nineteen-aught-something is still hanging in mid-air. It's being played, right now, in the Elysian Fields; if we close our eyes, we can get there in a moment, to watch the children sport upon the shore. And, once we're there, I doubt if any of us *will* care if we ever get back.

APPENDIX:
WHEN THE ARCHETYPAL MASK SLIPS

Aristotle called it recognition, and his chief example was Oedipus, revealed to both chorus and audience for the incestuous patricide that he really was. Ibsen had Nora Helmer reveal her true nature to his audience in *A Doll's House* when she told her husband Torvald she was "getting out of her costume." When Jonathan Swift could no longer keep a lid on his savage indignation, the mask of his persona would slip off and Swift would step out of character, delivering an angry jeremiad in his own unmistakable voice. One of the ways this happens in sport is when the individual who has been archetypally hidden by our need to mythify "comes out." Tonya Harding, we thought, was a scrappy little street kid, poor but talented, a very American hero, until she "came out" and showed us a ruthless competitor who may even have discussed murdering a rival. And then there is the horrific case of O.J. Simpson.

O.J. Simpson had been for decades a typical Apollonian. Even his nickname was healthy and wholesome. He was O.J., or just "Juice," O.J. of the broad smile and sweet disposition, O.J. the cheerful airport sprinter and innocently bumbling movie cop, good-natured O.J.—O.J. Simpson, who was then suddenly and credibly accused of deliberately hacking two young people to death, "deliberately" in both the sense of "premeditated" and in that of "methodical," since it took upwards of twenty wounds to dispatch one of his victims, who was, incidentally, attacked when his back was turned.

The first O.J. is clearly the O.J. of myth, the archetype and image, a figure wearing the smiling mask we have forced him to wear; the second, just as clearly, is the real Simpson, certainly guilty of at least one previous assault and now indicted for murder, the kid who grew up in the worst

153

ghetto in San Francisco. O.J. Simpson's mask hasn't just slipped, it's been *torn* off.

While cases like Harding's and Simpson's resemble those of more conventional pariahs like Joe Jackson and Eleanor Holm, it's important to recognize that both Jackson and Holm "fell" only in their roles as archetypes and solely within the confines of their mythic lives, and that they were punished exclusively by the organizations which insisted that they remain faithful to those archetypes. The "falls" of Jackson and Holm were not enmeshed with (or even particularly connected to) the way they behaved in the lives they led outside of their sports.

Not so with the cases of Harding and Simpson, where the individual wearing the mask turns out to have little or nothing to do with the archetypal image projected. In cases like these, the fans and the media have chosen a particularly unsuitable individual for the type, and now the Aristotelian shock of recognizing the truth becomes that much harder to bear. Harding, tough, little, and muscular, the Leo Gorcey of figure skating, had been assigned the "slot" of the courageous and productive Dionysiac, and we were dismayed to find that the real Tonya was a very destructive one instead. The case of O.J. was even worse—the image of a productive Apollonian was turned into that of a destructive Dionysiac at a stroke, like a medieval knight suddenly revealed to be a loathsome devil in disguise. In both cases, however, the crucial distinction remains that the revealed villains are shown as villains in real life. True, Harding is also the more conventional pariah, the betrayer of her sport, the rule-breaker, but an athlete who considers homicide and encourages assault with a deadly weapon has certainly gone on to become a villain "off the field," too. In Simpson's case, of course, the villainy was entirely unrelated to the sport.

What is particularly saddening here is the fact that the Apollonian O.J. was created by us, by the fans, and by our ambassadors, the media. For more than two decades we insisted that O.J. be the mild-mannered guy who lives next door and invites us over for barbecue and a couple of beers, and O.J. obliged. He even began to believe it, to believe in this artificially created, cosmetic second self, and there is pathetic evidence that he believes it still. In his note to his friend Robert Kardashian, Simpson said this: "Please think of the real O.J. and not this lost person." Simpson, of course, had it backwards; it's the violent "lost person" who is real. "O.J.," sadly, is a cosmetic mannequin, and only the mythical archetype.

Is O.J.'s story a "tragedy" as so many have said? Probably not. Joe Jackson, whose entire story is told within the archetypal framework of his sport, might be considered a tragic hero, but O.J.'s case straddles the worlds of myth and reality, and O.J. was a hero only in the myth created by fans and media. In reality he was always a fairly ordinary "lost person," and that person was always there, just particularly well costumed. Despite the obvious parallels with *Othello*—a play in which a heroic husband kills his wife and tries to kill his wife's lover, although wife and "lover" are both innocent—O.J. was no hero, not by a long shot, and this is true even if he is found to be innocent, since he has certainly been shown to be a persistent and even conventional wife-beater.

Finally, I would like to glance at what is easily the least palatable aspect of our role as mythmakers: our desire to vilify the hero who has let us down after we have made him into an archetypal figure, in the process setting standards for him which are beyond his capacity as a flawed individual.

I've already discussed how the media, and in particular Hughey Fullerton, actually invented stories to make Joe Jackson look worse than he may have been. In Simpson's case, the most scurrilous piece of journalism, no less offensive because it may have been unconscious rather than overt, was the cover of *Time* on June 27, 1994. It showed O.J.'s police mug shot, but the picture had been blurred and darkened by an artist, making O.J. look much blacker than he actually is.

Is this an editorial reference to Simpson's just-revealed "dark" side, or, worse, is it plain racism? Does the white power structure feel betrayed by this black athlete, a man they had accepted as one of their own, and are they now bluntly and unsubtly disowning him, emphasizing the blackness of his alleged sin by deepening that of his skin?

Further, does the blurring of Simpson's photograph stereotype him in a fresh way? Does the fuzzy image indicate that, far from considering him as a real individual at last, we are now only going to re-mythify O.J.?

To see how much darker and more blurred this picture is we need only look at *Newsweek*'s cover for the same week, which reproduces the same photo, but undoctored. It's quite clear from the *Time* cover that we have already begun to fit O.J. Simpson into another archetype (editors at *Time* said they had intended "an icon of tragedy" [4 July 1994]). In any case, we have begun to force him to wear a mask again, but this is a mask much, much different than the one we forced on him before.

WORKS CONSULTED AND CITED

Adams, Robert M., ed. *Utopia*. By Sir Thomas More. New York: Norton, 1992. 99-101.

Angell, Roger. *The Summer Game*. New York: Viking, 1972.

Barfield, Owen. "Dream, Myth, and Philosophical Double Vision." *Myths, Dreams and Religion*. Ed. Joseph Campbell. New York: Dutton, 1970. 211-24.

Becker, Ernest. *The Denial of Death*. New York: Free, 1973.

Berry, Barbara. *The Thoroughbreds*. Indianapolis: Bobbs, 1974.

Bjarkman, Peter C. "Bums' Lit." *The Cooperstown Review* 1 (1993): 54-70.

Bloom, Harold. *The Anxiety of Influence*. New York: Oxford UP, 1973.

Boswell, Thomas. "Why Is Baseball So Much Better Than Football?" *The Washington Post Magazine* 18 Jan. 1987: 29-31, 47.

Brosnan, Jim. "The Fantasy World of Baseball." *Sport Inside Out*. Ed. David L. Vanderwerken and Spencer K. Wertz. Ft. Worth: Texas Christian UP, 1985: 636-43.

Browne, Ray B. "Epilogue." *Heroes of Popular Culture*. Ed. Ray B. Browne, Marshall Fishwick, and Michael Marsden. Bowling Green, OH: Bowling Green State University Popular Press, 1972. 186-88.

Calhoun, Don. *Sports Culture and Personality*. West Point, NY: Leisure, 1981.

Campbell, Joseph. *The Hero with a Thousand Faces*. Princeton: Princeton UP, 1968.

Coffin, Tristram. *The Old Ball Game*. New York: Herder & Herder, 1971.

Connors, James. *Illustrated History of the Great Corbett-Sullivan Ring Battle*. Buffalo: privately printed, 1892.

Corbett, James J. *The Roar of the Crowd*. London: Phoenix, 1925.

Corum, Bill. *Off and Running*. New York: Holt, 1959.

Cozens, Frederick W., and Florence Scovil Stumpf. *Sports in American Life*. Chicago: U of Chicago P, 1953.

Cramer, Judith A., Jon E. Walker, and Leslie Rado. "Athletic Heroes and Heroines: The Role of the Press in Their Creation." *Journal of Sport Behavior* 4.4 (1984): 175-85.

Creamer, Robert. *Babe: The Legend Comes to Life*. New York: Penguin, 1983.

Dunne, Finley Peter. "On Baseball." *Mr. Dooley in Peace and War*. Boston: Ellis, 1898. 249-54.

Durant, John. *The Heavyweight Champions*. New York: Hastings, 1976.

Edwards, Harry. *Sociology of Sport*. Homewood, IL: Dorsey, 1973.

Faulkner, William. *Absalom, Absalom!* New York: Modern Library, 1936.

Folsom, F.E. "The Miscalled Good Old Days of the Umpire Baiter." *Baseball Magazine* 39 (Sept. 1927): 459-60.

Frazer, Sir James George. *The Golden Bough*. New York: Collier, 1963.

Gallico, Paul. *Farewell to Sport*. New York: Knopf, 1938.

Goldstein, Warren. "It Happens Every Spring." *Lingua Franca* June 1991: 26-29.

Gorn, Elliott J. *The Manly Art*. Ithaca: Cornell UP, 1986.

Greenberg, Eric Rolfe. *The Celebrant*. New York: Penguin, 1983.

Greenfield, Thomas A. *Work and the Work Ethic in American Drama, 1920-1970*. Columbia: U of Missouri P, 1982.

Grella, George. *Sport Inside Out*. Ed. David L. Vanderwerken and Spencer K. Wertz. Fort Worth: Texas Christian UP, 1985.

Gropman, Donald. *Say It Ain't So, Joe!* Boston: Little, 1979.

Gutman, Herbert G. *Work, Culture and Society in Industrializing America*. New York: Vintage, 1966.

Guttmann, Allen. *Sports Spectators*. New York: Columbia UP, 1986.

Harris, Mark. *Bang the Drum Slowly*. New York: Knopf, 1960.

Higgs, Robert J. *Sports: A Reference Guide*. Westport, CT: Greenwood, 1982.

Huizinga, Johan. *Homo Ludens*. Boston: Beacon, 1950.

Ingraham, Jim. "The Magnificent Career and Tragic Death of Addie Joss." *Baseball History* 1.2 (Summer 1986): 15-31.

James, Bill. *The Bill James Historical Baseball Abstract*. New York: Villard, 1986.

Joyce, James. *Finnegans Wake*. New York: Viking, 1939.

Jung, Carl Gustav. *Man and His Symbols*. New York: Dell, 1964.

———. *Two Essays on Analytical Psychology*. New York: Meridian, 1956.

Keenan, Francis. "The Athletic Contest as a 'Tragic' Form of Art." *The Philosophy of Sport*. Ed. Robert G. Osterhoudt. Springfield, IL: Thomas, 1973. 309-26.

Klapp, Orrin E. *Heroes, Villains and Fools*. Englewood Cliffs: Prentice-Hall, 1962.

———. *Symbolic Leaders*. Chicago: Aldine, 1964.

Lardner, Rex. *The Legendary Champions*. New York: American Heritage, 1972.

Leach, Edmund R. "Genesis as Myth." *Myth and Cosmos*. Ed. John Middleton. Garden City: Natural History, 1967. 1-13.

Leeming, David Adams. *The World of Myth*. New York: Oxford UP, 1990.

Lehmann-Haupt, Christopher. "Books of the Times." *New York Times* 25 Feb. 1988: C29.

Lenk, Hans. "Herculean 'Myth' Aspects of Athletes." *Sport Inside Out*. Ed. David L. Vanderwerken and Spencer K. Wertz. Ft. Worth: Texas Christian UP, 1985. 435-47.

Leverenz, David. *The Language of Puritan Feeling*. New Brunswick: Rutgers UP, 1980.

Lipsky, Richard. *How We Play the Game*. Boston: Beacon, 1981.

McCallum, John D. *The World Heavyweight Boxing Championship*. Radnor, PA: Chilton, 1974.

Messenger, Christian. "Introduction to Sport and the Spirit of Play in American Fiction." *American Sport Culture*. Ed. Wiley Lee Umphlett. Lewisburg: Bucknell UP, 1985. 197-211.

Neumann, Erich. *The Great Mother: An Analysis of the Archetype*. Princeton: Princeton UP, 1964.

Nietzsche, Friedrich. *The Birth of Tragedy*. Garden City: Anchor, 1956.

Novak, Michael. "American Sports, American Virtues." *American Sport Culture*. Ed. Wiley Lee Umphlett. Lewisburg: Bucknell UP, 1985, 34-49.

———. *The Joy of Sports*. New York: Basic, 1976.

O'Connor, Gerard. "Where Have you Gone, Joe DiMaggio?" *Heroes of Popular Culture*. Ed. Ray B. Browne, Marshall Fishwick, and Michael Marsden. Bowling Green, OH: Bowling Green State University Popular Press, 1972. 86-99.

Oriard, Michael. *Dreaming of Heroes.* Chicago: Nelson-Hall, 1982.

___. *Sporting with the Gods.* New York: Cambridge UP, 1991.

Progoff, Ira. *Jung's Psychology and Its Social Meaning.* Garden City: Doubleday, 1973.

Propp, Vladimir. *Morphology of the Folktale.* Austin: U of Texas P, 1970.

Rank, Otto. *The Myth of the Birth of the Hero.* New York: Vintage, 1959.

Ritter, Lawrence S. *The Glory of Their Times.* New York: Morrow, 1984.

Roberts, Randy. *Papa Jack.* New York: Free, 1983.

Ruskin, John. "The Pathetic Fallacy." *Selections and Essays.* New York: Scribner's, 1918.

Said, Edward. "Criticism/Self-Criticism." *Lingua Franca.* Feb./Mar. 1992: 37-43.

Seymour, Harold. *Baseball: the Golden Age.* New York: Oxford UP, 1971.

Slusher, Howard S. *Man, Sport and Existence.* Philadelphia: Lea & Febiger, 1967.

Smith, Garry. "The Sport Hero: An Endangered Species." *Play, Games and Sports.* Ed. Janet C. Harris and Roberta J. Park. Champaign, IL: Human Kinetics, 1983. 107-22.

Smith, Leverett. "Ty Cobb, Babe Ruth and the Changing Image of the Athletic Hero." *Heroes of Popular Culture.* Ed. Ray B. Browne, Marshall Fishwick, and Michael Marsden. Bowling Green, OH: Bowling Green State University Popular Press. 73-85.

Souriau, Étienne. *The 200,000 Dramatic Situations.* Paris: Flammarion, 1950.

Strauss, William, and Neil Howe. *Generations.* New York: Morrow, 1991.

Stump, Al. "Ty Cobb's Wild Ten-Month Fight to Live." *The Baseball Reader.* Ed. Charles Einstein. New York: McGraw, 1983. 387-412.

Stump, Al, and Ty Cobb. *My Life in Baseball.* Garden City: Doubleday, 1961.

Thorn, John. "The Father of Baseball?" *Elysian Fields Quarterly* 11.1 (1992): 85-91.

Umphlett, Wiley Lee. *American Sport Culture.* Lewisburg: Bucknell UP, 1975.

____. *The Sporting Myth and the American Experience.* Lewisburg: Bucknell UP, 1975.

Unamuno, Miguel de. *The Tragic Sense of Life.* New York: Dover, 1954.

Veblen, Thorstein. *The Theory of the Leisure Class.* New York: Penguin, 1979.

Voigt, David. *America Through Baseball.* Chicago: Nelson-Hall, 1976.

____. *American Baseball. Vol. 2. From the Commissioner to Continental Expansion.* Norman, OK: U of Oklahoma P, 1970.

Weber, Max. *The Protestant Ethic and the Spirit of Capitalism.* New York: Scribner's, 1977.

Weston, Jessie L. *From Ritual to Romance.* Garden City: Anchor, 1957.

Index